PRAISE FOR NINA AMIR

"Change doesn't happen because you wrote something. It happens because you built trust before you asked for attention, because you saw your readers clearly enough to meet them where they are, and because you cared enough to do the hard work of actually understanding how transformation works. This isn't a book about writing. It's a book about mattering. The writing is just the tool." —Seth Godin, author of *This is Marketing*

"In *Change the World, One Book at a Time*, Nina Amir has brought authors a masterpiece of empowerment. Authors will learn step by step how to harness and direct their passions and expertise to effectuate positive change in the world." —Mark Coker, founder of Smashwords, Chief Strategy Officer, Draft2Digital, host of the *Smart Author* Podcast

"Bookstores are filled with books that entertain and inform. Books that change lives and the world are harder to find, and many of them don't ever have an impact. This book makes it possible for writers to understand their audiences, build communities around their causes, and become what Nina Amir calls 'Authors of Change.' This is a must-read if you are writing for change." —Scott Lorenz, Westwind Book Marketing

"Writing reaches its greatest potential when it goes beyond the simple concerns and thoughts of the writer and expands into the richness of our complex world, and Nina Amir's Change the World One Book at a Time shows us exactly how it is done. This unique writing guide is an essential tool for those who want to write books that will transform and change." —Dinty W. Moore, author of *The Mindful Writer*

"Change the World One Book at a Time is perfect for anyone with a meaningful message or timely topic that you're ready to put out into the world. Full of practical guidance and invaluable support, Nina Amir provides change makers with essential tools to make a bold impact with their words."

—Jordan Rosenfeld, author of the novel *Fallout* and *The Sound of Story: Developing Voice & Tone in Writing*

"Many authors set out to spark change—but without the right strategy, even the most powerful idea can fall flat. In Change the World One Book at a Time, Nina Amir hands cause-driven writers the blueprint they've been missing. From crafting a message that truly moves readers to building the community that turns a book into a movement, this guide covers the real work of impact. If you have a mission and the motivation to share it, this book shows you how to make sure your words don't just land—they inspire action and create lasting change." —Penny C. Sansevieri, CEO of Author Marketing Experts and author of *The Amazon Author Formula*

"Change the World One Book at a Time shows aspiring 'Authors of Change' how to craft books that inspire transformation, build movements, and move readers to action - and make a huge impact along the way. Nina's book is a must-read for leaders, coaches, activists, and visionaries who dream of leaving a lasting legacy through the written word." —Rusty Shelton, bestselling author of *Mastering the New Media Landscape: Embrace the Micromedia Mindset* and Chairman of Zilker Media

"If you're passionate about writing a book with the potential to improve people's lives, and you're looking for an indispensable guide that covers all the ins and outs of writing and publishing a transformational work, you'll want Nina Amir's Change the World One Book at a Time by your side." — Martha Alderson, author of *Boundless Creativity: a Spiritual Guide for Overcoming Self-doubt, Emotional Traps and other Creative Blocks*

"Ready to create a legacy? If you're looking to write and publish a book that empowers your future readers to transform some aspect of their lives, their community and the wider world, Nina Amir's Change the World One Book at a Time is your resource! Amir's book begins with 'A better time to make a difference has never existed.' With this inspirational orientation and her decades of experience in publishing and coaching, you'll find the guidance, wisdom and time-tested strategies to write, publish and market a book that has the impact you dream of." —Lisa Tener, author of *Breathe. Write. Breathe.*

"The world needs change, and who better to inspire that change than writers? Change the World One Book at a Time provides a comprehensive guide for any writer who wants to make a difference with their words." —Rick Frishman, Publisher and bestselling author of 19 books, including *Guerrilla Marketing for Writers*

"Change the World One Book at a Time: Make a Positive and Meaningful Difference with Your Words by Nina Amir can change the world with many books at the same time. It is the right book at the right time and needed more than ever around the world. It's an essential, state-of-the-art guide to writing, publishing, and building a career for all writers. Change the World will help librarians, booksellers, parents, and teachers at all levels. It should be adapted for workbooks and teaching at all levels. An inspiring legacy, the book fulfills Miss. Amir's hopes for it and deserves all of the success it earns." —Michael Larsen, coauthor *How to Write a Book Proposal, 5th Edition*, with Jodi Rein; Cofounder, San Francisco Writing Conference

Each chapter is a step-by-step guide with outlines, charts, and deep inquiry into your purpose and passion to inspire others with your book. Nina's personal examples of her own growth and development show us 'you can do this too!' I found many suggestions that will be helpful as I write my next book."

—Linda Joy Myers, founder of the National Association of Memoir Writers, author of *Don't Call Me Mother*

"For writers who wish to make a real difference, this comprehensive guide is a must-read. As author Amir acknowledges in the first chapter of this book, attempting to become an author of change can feel hugely daunting—but 'someone needs your book.' In Change the World One Book at a Time, she leads (and cheerleads) you through every step of the journey—from clarifying your message for yourself to putting it on the page in a way that will most effectively reach an audience—making what might otherwise feel like an overwhelming challenge accessible for all." —Brooke Warner, author of *Write on, Sisters!* and publisher of She Writes Press

CHANGE THE WORLD ONE BOOK AT A TIME

NINA AMIR

Published by Books That Save Lives, an imprint of Jim Dandy Publishing, LLC

Cover Design: Carmen Fortunato
Artist Photo: Sari Singerman

Jim Dandy Publishing
6252 Peach Avenue
Van Nuys, CA 91411
info@jimdandypublishing.com

For bulk orders, special quantities, course adoptions, and corporate sales, please email info@jimdandypublishing.com

ISBN: (print) 978-1963667295, (ebook) 978-1963667301

BISAC: LAN002000, LAN005000, LAN005060

Printed in the United States of America

This book is dedicated to every person who feels the calling to make the world a better place. May this book support your efforts to impact lives and create change.

CONTENTS

Foreword   xiii
Introduction: An Invitation   xvii

1. Author the Change You Want to See in the World   1
2. Clarify Your Purpose   13

PART I
How to Embody Change   35

3. Understand Change   37
4. Become an Author of Change   67
5. Be the Messenger and the Message   91

PART II
How to Inspire Change   117

6. Build Engaged Platforms and Communities   119
7. Make a Difference Online   138
8. Motivate with Creative and Traditional Tools   159

PART III
How to Author Change   179

9. Prepare to Write a Transformational Book   181
10. Write a Book that Makes a Difference   207
    Conclusion: Time for Action   232

Acknowledgments   239
About the Author   241
About the Publisher   243

FOREWORD

You've purchased this book and you've started to read. Dear reader, lucky you. You're about to have a transformative experience. You're about to discover that the book you're wanting to write (or that you're writing) can't be authored by anyone but you. You're about to find out just how sacred an act writing your book really is. And perhaps most important, if you keep going to the very end of this book, you'll finish knowing that you—through the vehicle that is your book—have the power to effect profound change.

I've traveled in the same writerly circles with Nina Amir for fifteen years, and I know a fellow author advocate when I see one. Nina's mission is singular and focused: to support you to write the book you are meant to write. For 35 years, Nina has been supporting people, whether they think of themselves as writers or not, to fulfill their potential as creators and leaders through the books they write.

Nina knows, deep in her bones, that the act of writing, and eventually becoming an author, is among the most transformative things a person can do. The only way to come to this kind of deep knowing is through years of witnessing what happens when someone takes up the pen (or takes to the keyboard) and writes. And writes and writes and writes—until all of those cumulative words become a book, and that person becomes an author. Once that happens, as anyone who's an author knows, your world changes. With your book, you have a conversation starter. You have transformed from having been someone with something to say to someone with a message to share. You become an expert, and doors start to open to you.

It sounds nice, and it is. It's also not an easy road you set off on when you decide you want to write a book. In my own work as a publisher, a coach, and an editor, I marvel at the number of obstacles writers must face and overcome on the journey to becoming a published author. It's easy to get derailed, lost, scared, overwhelmed. There are those nasty inner critics to deal with, too. We compare ourselves, let perfect be the enemy of good, and start to doubt our purpose or our capacity. We start to think, *You know what? Someone else has already written a similar book, and it's probably better than mine will be.* We start to waver and question whether we're really the person to write this book, after all. We undermine ourselves, and we lose steam.

But—once you've decided you want to write a book, the idea of it is hard to shake. So it inevitably resurfaces. It nibbles at you. You will start to think to yourself, *You know what—I really should write that book. I am the right person, after all. I think I'm going to do it.*

You may be familiar with this push and pull, and it can go on for years. Which is why a book like *Change the World One Book at a Time* is so important. It exists to connect you to purpose, and to support you to align with and embrace your writerly identity. This is Nina Amir's brilliant framework for this book—that being and becoming a writer is an identity, and once you embrace it, it's part of you. That you are the only person who can write your book becomes your destiny when you see things in this new light. And Nina is persistent and consistent in her encouragement that you have something powerful to share with the world. No matter what, you do.

Once you embrace your writerly identity, you'll start to think of yourself as a writer, and that's helpful. Even still, writers easily lose track of purpose. We know we want to write, but things get muddied along the way. Staying connected to the big purpose at the center of this book—that you are a cultural contributor, not just content creator—will propel you all the way to the finish line.

Most of us want to make a difference. We want to leave a legacy. We want to help others. We want to contribute something meaningful. We want to be change-makers. Whatever your reason for coming to the page, you will connect to purposes in a powerful way in the pages of this book, and you'll see how story, self-expression, and the written word will steady you and keep you grounded in what you say you want to do.

Writing is more than a vehicle to share the stories of our lives, our experience, and our expertise. It's our birthright, too, and a gift to others. Let *Change the World One Book at a Time* be your lighthouse, a book you will turn to again and again whenever you get untethered from your why. Let Nina Amir's words be a guide back to yourself, and back to your inner knowing that part of the reason you're here, living this life, is to write your own book that will change the world.

—Brooke Warner, Publisher of She Writes Press and author of ***Write On, Sisters!***

INTRODUCTION:
AN INVITATION

When passion meets purpose, inspiration sparks. You feel moved to action. Since you opened this book, inspired action for you means writing a book that makes a positive and meaningful difference in the world. You want to write a book that motivates readers to internal or external change, solves a problem, or improves a situation.

You want to become an *Author of Change.*

A book can wield enormous power if read by the masses. That's why historically books have been feared, banned, and destroyed by those who wish to stifle change. Your book can have such power, too, but first, you must free your idea from inside your head, mold it into a marketable manuscript, and get it into readers' hands.

Sounds simple enough. However, many people experience the path to *successful* authorship as a long, arduous, lonely, and overwhelming, journey. But it doesn't have to be. In fact, you can have a totally different experience.

In these pages, you will find the comfort that comes from knowing you are not alone. I'm here, and so are the many writers around the world who are writing books that, once published, will inspire and motivate change. Additionally, whether you are new to writing and feel unsure of where to begin or are an author who wants additional strategies to help your book have greater impact, you'll receive the advice you need within these pages. I've included details on every step of the journey, including how to understand and motivate change; share your message; create an audience; conceptualize a marketable book; write consistently, complete a manuscript with the potential to move readers toward transformation; and determine your best publishing option. This book is intended to fuel your sense of purpose and provide you with clear strategies and action steps to fulfill it.

Since early adulthood, my favorite books have been those that inspired me in some way. I craved the ones that helped me understand myself or the world, motivated me to think big, or helped me solve a problem. I dreamed of writing such books myself.

I've built my career on inspiring writers to become successful authors and publish books that make a difference. I wrote this book to encourage people like you to become Authors of Change—to publish books that transform lives, communities, organizations, countries, and the world.

In fact, this book serves as an invitation to join my movement. To accept, commit to writing and publishing your transformational book, thereby sharing your message of change.

Kabbalah, the ancient Jewish mystical tradition, teaches that it is our job as humans to repair what is broken in the world. We do this with acts of kindness, pursuit of social justice, and sacred actions that fix the broken pieces. Those pieces could be in individuals or their lives, communities, organizations, systems, or the world at large.

Writing is a sacred act.

The world needs repair. You know it. I know it. You hold the power to repair it with your words and wisdom. The book you write and publish transmits that power to individuals who join you in making a difference.

Do your sacred part to repair even a tiny part of the world. Become an Author of Change.

1

AUTHOR THE CHANGE YOU
WANT TO SEE IN THE WORLD

True, This...

The pen is mightier than the sword...Take away the sword—States can be saved without it!

— EDWARD BULWER-LYTTON, *RICHELIEU; OR
THE CONSPIRACY*

A better time to make a difference has never existed. Look around—at your life, friends and family, community, organization, or country. Ample causes exist, and you've chosen one you believe in. Marching, making phone calls, striking, and other forms of peaceful protest provide effective ways to motivate decisive action. Additionally, you can get on your soap box and blast your transformational message to those you encounter, using influence and persuasion to move them toward new behaviors.

There is another way: *Write a book that makes a positive and meaningful difference in the world.*

Don't fight *against* what you do not like or the problems you know need solving. Instead, fight *for* the change you want to inspire, and do so with written words. *Author the change you want to see in the world.*

You've heard it before: "The pen is mightier than the sword." It's time for you to release your words as weapons for good, tools to fix the brokenness, bandages for the unhealed wounds. Whether you write fiction or nonfiction, the words you put on the page impact those who read them.

It's time to take up this rallying cry: *Author change!*

What is an Author of Change?

Authors of Change are people from all walks of life—writers, coaches, healers, conscious entrepreneurs, visionaries, experts, parents, and activists—who choose to write books that make a difference. They fall into one or more of the following categories:

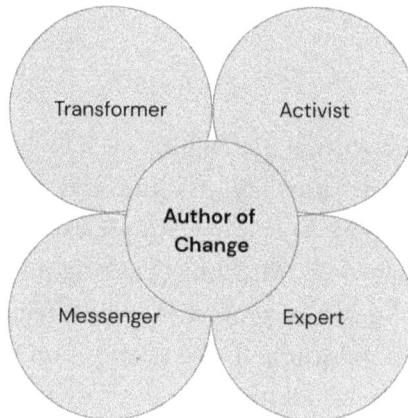

A **Transformer** feels spiritually or morally called to create change. You have an inner need to transform lives or the world and operate with a strong sense of higher calling. You know your message, cause, or movement is something you are meant to pursue. It's your sacred work during this lifetime to positively transform people, situations, and conditions.

An **Activist** is motivated by injustice, problems, or broken situations that need repair. You feel driven by your values and a strong sense of right versus wrong. You sense the ailing places of the world deeply in your core, and they motivate you to heal them.

A **Messenger** knows that sharing knowledge and experience provides a means of service. You might sense that your personal story has transformative power. And you feel service is your purpose and the highest act of giving.

An **Expert** is a thought leader or authority in a subject area or industry. You feel a strong urge to offer your knowledge and make a difference. You know your expertise and experience can help others, and you want to give back and use your influence for good.

According to Brendon Burchard, *New York Times* bestselling author of *The Millionaire Messenger,* experts also fall into the following categories:

- The results expert—someone who has knowledge others don't yet possess.
- The research expert—someone who researches a topic to become an expert.
- The role model—someone trusted, respected, admired, followed, and listened to by others.

However, all Authors of Change have one thing in common: They feel called to write a book that inspires and motivates change. They want to make a positive and meaningful difference with their words.

The Power of a Book to Make a Difference

Throughout history, authors have left a legacy of change. Consider famous transformational books, like *The Republic* by Plato, *The Communist Manifesto* by Karl Marx and Friedrich Engels, *Common Sense* by Thomas Paine, *I Ching* by Fu Xi, *The Prince* by Niccolo Machiavelli, *Walden* by Henry David Thoreau, and *Uncle Tom's Cabin* by Harriett Beecher Stowe.

The list of transformational books is tremendously long, and each person feels inspired by a different author or topic. Maybe you have read a book that altered your life, like *Silent Spring* by Rachel Carson, *Think and Grow Rich* by Napoleon Hill, *High Performance Habits* by Brendon Burchard, or *A New Earth* by Eckhart Tolle. Jeff Bezos, founder of Amazon, was most influenced by *Remains of the Day* by Kazuo Ishiguro. Will Smith, Madonna, and Pharrell Williams all credit *The Alchemist* by Paulo Coelho for changing their lives. Sergey Brin, creator of Google, was impacted by reading *Surely You're Joking, Mr. Feynman!* by the Nobel-winning theoretical physicist Richard Feynman. And former President Ronald Reagan claimed two books directed his life, *That Printer of Udell's* by Harold Bell Wright and *Witness* by Whittaker Chambers.

A Multitude of Ways to Share Your Message

The ability to share written messages dates to the use of hieroglyphs. To record and disseminate information, humans took up the use of papyrus, waxed tablets, clay, wood, slate, parchment, and amate—all precursors to the innovation we know as paper. Yet even using paper to share information widely required painstaking hours of scribing.

The invention of the printing press expanded our ability to reach an audience. The reproduction of manuscripts morphed from a time-consuming and laborious manual process to a quick and effective mechanical one that allowed for mass production of printed books. The printing press became the catalyst for societal and cultural transformations that began in the sixteenth century, such as the Industrial Revolution, the rise of nationalism in Europe, and the use of perspective in art. Albert Eisenstein regarded the printing press as an agent for the development of the Renaissance, the Protestant Reformation, and the advance of modern scientific thought.

Then came the Internet. In early 2025, there were approximately 5.56 billion internet users worldwide, representing 68 percent of the global population. The Internet altered how we share essential messages, influence people, advocate for causes, and start movements. The more people connected via the Internet, the greater anyone's ability to impact a target market as an Author of Change.

Books are shared on the World Wide Web, too. As you build a community around your transformational book, your message could go viral. The next book or hashtag shared by millions could be one related to your cause or calling. At the very least, promoting your book on the Internet might result in more readers. That means more people receive the opportunity to learn about and apply the transformational strategies you suggest. Each person who achieves personal transformation impacts those in their circle of influence. In this manner, you and your book create a transformational ripple effect that can extend worldwide.

Let us not forget e-books and e-readers, two more technological advances that make it easier to author change today than ever before. E-books removed a barrier to authoring change. No longer do books have to be printed and distributed in physical form, an expensive and often lengthy process. Instead, an author can publish a book digitally and make it available immediately to a global readership at little manufacturing cost and without shipping expense.

More recently, audiobooks have become the fastest growing trend in the publishing industry and, as such, represent another opportunity to share transformational messages. The increase in audiobook consumption can be correlated with the increased number of people spending time online since audiobooks are often purchased via digital downloads. That's good news for Authors of Change; it means your book can be consumed either with eyes or ears, increasing its potential impact.

By now you realize that today you can take advantage of a multitude of ways to share your message, cause, or mission effectively and quickly with people worldwide. Your book can be offered in multiple formats, and you can use a variety of online tools to effectively reach millions of people around the globe in minutes. For these reasons, the potential reach and impact of your book is far greater than ever before.

Your Pen Is Mighty

Today, we need another advance that can be brought about by writers serving as change agents: We need people like you to link available technology to sorely needed solutions. You need no expertise to look at the world and exclaim, "We need change...now!" Anyone can see that transformation is a necessity—almost everywhere and in every situation. But it's easy to fall into apathy and a sense of powerlessness. You might tell yourself, "I can't make a difference. I'm just one person. The problem is too large." or "I'm nobody...no one knows who I am. I won't be able to influence anyone or anything. Few people, if any, will read my book."

Here's the truth of the matter: If you have a solution to even one small problem, you can make a significant difference. If you have the answer to just one question or a strategy that works for you in a specific situation, you can have a positive impact. This fact is especially true for writers.

This moment in time is filled with opportunities for writers to repair even a small piece of what's broken in the world. With the technology available, you can choose a vehicle and set about impacting your target audience. You no longer need to wait for permission or ask a gatekeeper to get your message heard by those who need it most.

However, in order to author change, you must possess more than the ability to put words on paper or complete the publishing process. You need more than passion, purpose, inspiration, motivation, a cause, or a sense of calling. You need the courage and energy to take bold and consistent action as well.

Specifically, becoming an Author of Change requires completing a three-step process.

1. Activate change in your life and understand how to inspire it in the lives of others.
2. Motivate others to join your movement or take different action.
3. Write a transformational book and get it in the hands of your readers.

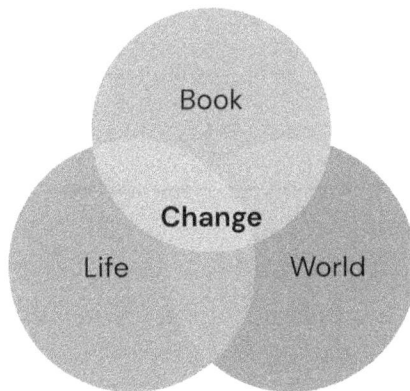

This book takes you through all three steps. Part One focuses on understanding how you change and how to inspire others to change. Part Two provides an in-depth look at how to create a community around your movement—people who want to purchase your book and follow your transformational advice. And Part Three takes you through the process of completing the manuscript for a book that can change lives and the world. All three parts are essential if you want to write a book that can change the world. Let me explain why.

First, your life must become a reflection of the transformation about which you want to write. You must become someone who can lead a movement and inspire others to join it. You must understand change and how to motivate people to do things differently, and you need to transform yourself into an author.

Second, you need to take your mission or cause into the world. You have to create a community of like-minded people eager and willing to join your movement, try your strategies or solutions, or behave in ways you propose. You initiate your mission by inviting people to become part of it via your website, online activity, speaking, and by any other means that gathers interested people around your cause. Your community gives you the ability to market your book effectively before and after publication—and for many years after.

Third, you must write a book that will sell. If it sells, it gets read, and the impact of your message grows. Additionally, you must compose a manuscript that moves readers to take the action you recommended.

Only with these three pieces in place can you successfully author change. While these steps don't have to be completed in chronological order, your book stands a better chance of success if you have already created transformation in your life or that of others, stepped into a leadership role, and created an audience ready and willing to purchase the book. Also, you'll write a better book—one targeted at the needs of your reader—after time spent with and in your community. That experience informs your book's content.

Step Up and Into Your Best Writing Self

The world needs people like you. That's why now is the time to write your book—not later. You feel the intense internal push to make a difference. Personal, business, or world circumstances have increased the intensity of your desire to act. Sometimes you think your book must be released this moment...or it will be too late.

You may hesitate. But think of all the reluctant leaders throughout history, such as Moses, Jonah, George Washington, Dwight D. Eisenhower, Thomas Beckett, and King George VI. Like them, you may believe you don't know enough, have too little experience, lack leadership ability, or have no expert status. You may think you communicate haltingly, which makes you an unqualified candidate to share an important message. After all, who are you to lead a movement or suggest new strategies, right?

In reality, who are you *not* to lead a movement? As Marianne Williamson so aptly wrote in *A Return to Love: Reflections on the Principles of A Course in Miracles*: "Our deepest fear is not that we are inadequate. Our deepest fear is that we are powerful beyond measure. It is our light, not our darkness that most frightens us. We ask ourselves, 'Who am I to be brilliant, gorgeous, talented, fabulous?' Actually, who are you not to be? ...Your playing small does not serve the world..."

I get it. Like you, I have struggled with the same negative thoughts and beliefs, ones that stopped me in my tracks while writing. I have lacked courage. But here's what I know: You are the right person to share your message. You know this, too. It may feel egotistical to say that to yourself, but no one else can tell your story, provide your solution, or inspire others in the same way. Only you can write your book. So, admit it: *It is your book to write.*

You also know you need to write the book and get it into readers' hands sooner rather than later. After all, what would happen—or not happen—if you never wrote your book? Who would you fail to impact, and what would be the result of that inaction? Do these people need your book in two years or right now?

Realizing the necessity of writing your book doesn't mean you should rush the process. In fact, the opposite is true, as successful authorship does not happen overnight. Take each step outlined in this book deliberately, carefully, and patiently. Little by little, step into being a leader and change agent, build your community, and produce a viable manuscript.

As you do so, remember: *Someone needs your book.* More than likely, many people need to read your book. In fact, they want and seek the inspiration and specific strategies you can provide. Each time you hesitate, stammer, or question the value you offer, you fail to provide the information they seek and force them to continue searching for the tips, tools, and answers necessary for transformation.

I know becoming an Author of Change feels like a big, scary, and demanding task. However, the moment you take even one small-but-bold action toward completing your manuscript and publishing your book, you possess the courage to continue. You need only start.

How long ago did the idea for your book pop into your head? When did your passion and purpose collide, leaving you feeling inspired to action? Yesterday? A year ago? Two, three, four (or more) years ago? Don't feel bad about yourself because you have not written or published your book yet. And don't allow disappointment in yourself or a belief that you have already failed stop you from authoring change.

Not this time. Not now.

Do something different—change yourself. Take bold and inspired action. Be an Author of Change.

The Battle Cry

It's time to take your pen—or keyboard—and use it to effect change. Join the ranks of people like then-fifteen-year-old Greta Thunberg, who sat on the steps of the Swedish parliament, following a summer of wildfires and sky-high temperatures in her home country. Her one bold action not only called attention to the need for climate change but quickly influenced millions of adults and young people alike. She went on to write *No One is Too Small to Make a Difference* and *The Climate Book: The Facts and The Solutions.*

Take a stand. Put your stake in the ground. Commit yourself to producing a book that wields the power to bring attention to important issues, ease people's pain, and provide solutions to the world's ills. Allow your words to become tools of meaningful positive change and touch millions of people around the world. For instance, follow in the footsteps of the committed and courageous young survivors of the shooting at Marjory Stoneman Douglas High School, who produced *Parkland Speaks.*

Consider the difference made by those who write bestselling self-help, personal development, and spiritual growth books. For example, Eckhart Tolle's *The Power of Now,* which helps readers get in touch with their thoughts and how destructive they can be, has been translated into fifty-two languages and has sold 12 million copies. His second book, *A New Earth,* which has been called a spiritual manifesto for a better way of life and building a better world, was picked up by Oprah Winfrey's book club and impacted people all around the world.

Numerous authors have inspired transformation in their readers. For example, Paulo Coelho's *The Alchemist* has sold over 65 million copies. This allegorical novel, which tells the story of a young shepherd's pursuit of treasure and the importance of following one's heart and dreams while paying attention to the journey, has been called one of the bestselling self-help books of all time. Louise L.

Hay's *You Can Heal Your Life* was published in 1984 and sold over 50 million copies; it remains on the list of the top self-improvement books ever published. Her book helps its readers navigate the mind-body connection and understand the underlying mental and emotional causes of illnesses. Of course, *Think and Grow Rich* by Napoleon Hill, which sold over 80 million copies, sits at the top of the list of bestselling books. By interviewing business moguls, he identified key laws and habits that drive success. Your name and book title could one day be found on a list of authors who have inspired change, too.

For eons, different spiritual traditions have relied on the power of personal stories. Every religion speaks of the power of words, as do personal growth, psychology, and Law of Attraction practitioners. Indeed, your words provide the means to change many.

Whether you see yourself as a Transformer, Activist, Messenger, or Expert—no matter what inspires and motivates you to write a change-related book, be courageous. Take bold action, even if that means changing yourself so you can change the world with your book. Use your words for good, for repair.

Write! Publish! Author change! Make that your battle cry. Then charge forward, and *author the change you want to see in the world.*

2

CLARIFY YOUR PURPOSE

"No man or woman is an island. To exist just for yourself is meaningless. You can achieve the most satisfaction when you feel related to some greater purpose in life, something greater than yourself."

— DENIS WAITLEY

Why have you chosen to inspire and motivate change? Change agents feel passionate about their causes, but passion alone is not enough to create transformation or write a book. You need a clear and strong sense of *purpose* to drive you forward. Your desire to make a difference pushes you to solve, rather than complain about, the problems you see in the world and to help heal, rather than ignore, human pain and suffering. You know the difference you want to make, and you may even have tried to inspire change already. However, the clearer you become about your purpose—the *reason* you want to work for this change—the higher the likelihood you'll achieve that desired result.

Now, your purpose has inspired you to write a book. Ideally, you and your book share the same purpose, because an aligned purpose exponentially increases the possibility of both succeeding.

Each writer's purpose is unique. To uncover your motives and determine the results you hope to accomplish takes deep reflection and honesty. Once clarified, though, your purpose guides your actions. When you tie it to your writing, purpose leads you to the book you are meant to write and others are waiting to read.

You might consider your purpose a *calling* or refer to it as a *cause*. Maybe you want to start a *movement*. Or you may feel compelled or have a gut feeling—perhaps it feels like a push from the universe or your higher self—to do something meaningful and positive with your life. The Still Small Voice whispers to you daily, "You can make a difference. It's your time to contribute."

You've listened and tried to make sense of this message. Maybe you previously tried to respond with actions that didn't create the desired results, but you know this is your work to do, your repair to make. Now you are here, considering writing a book as a way to heed the calling and make a difference.

If you are first and foremost a writer, you may not consider yourself a change agent, activist, or someone with a cause or movement. Yet you do want to inspire change, maybe with a self-help or how-to book. Reach deep inside yourself, and from a place of authenticity, connection, and faith, discover your purpose. Your desire to make a difference by writing a book serves as a smoldering ember. When you can name your purpose, you blow on the ember and encourage a flame to burst forth. The warmth and glow of this fire naturally attract your readers, and as a result, you create change.

On the other hand, many writers have clear reasons for writing their books. If you fall into this group, your strong sense of purpose already serves as your North Star. Use it to navigate the process of becoming an author.

Whether you see yourself primarily as a change agent or a writer, an emotionally charged reason to write for change significantly increases your chances of successfully writing and publishing a book. Your purpose ensures you don't get partway into writing your manuscript and then flounder. When your Big Why comes through clearly in your writing, readers take notice. Plus, your conviction helps you overcome challenges that might threaten completion of the book.

Every Author of Change Has a Purpose

Previously, you may not have called your reason for writing a book *your purpose*. Nor may you have been able to express it concisely. However, the ability to verbalize your purpose to your target audience, the people most interested in the change you want to propose, serves as a powerful tool.

Specifically, you need to be able to clearly articulate your purpose as it relates to your book. That skill allows you to communicate to potential readers why they want to read the book. You need the ability to boldly, passionately, and confidently offer a succinct purpose statement that compels people to take notice and action.

If you feel clear about the change you want to inspire, you know your purpose. Awesome! You are deeply connected to your desire to make a difference; you have identified an issue and know what you want to specifically accomplish with your book.

If you feel uncertain of your purpose, you need to find a "Big Why"—a reason you resonate with emotionally. Many of my clients have book ideas with the potential to make a difference in the world or in readers' lives. But some of them still don't have a clear idea of why they want to write the book and are disinclined to believe they—or their book—can influence anything. It's challenging to step out as an Author of Change while lacking confidence or suffering from impostor syndrome.

Know this: If you want to write a book that inspires change, you feel a sense of purpose. Maybe you just haven't uncovered it or arrived at clarity about it, but it's there. Now—before you write your book—identify your purpose and learn to state it explicitly. Then you will become confident in your ability to write the book.

Remember: Someone needs your book and is waiting for it. No matter how often they search, they don't see it on any bookstore shelf. Maybe, like them, you have searched for that same book but not found it. Keep that person in mind, and your purpose will become clearer and your commitment to writing the book stronger. You will know deep inside that you must write this book. In fact, only you *can* write it.

Find Your Purpose

You can find your purpose in many ways. Start by determining what type of Author of Change you are or want to be.

Maybe you possess expertise in a particular area, and your purpose exists there. You are an Expert and sense that you can make a difference if you share what you know. You'd like to be of service to others who want to excel in the same area. Similarly, your purpose might be connected to your profession and may give you a strong desire to change something within your industry. You might sense it's your time to give back—to use your knowledge and expertise to help others.

Perhaps you've had some unique life experiences you'd like to share, and therein lies your purpose. As a Messenger, you realize other people can learn from your story of how you overcame obstacles to success. You believe you suffered or struggled so you could inspire others to believe they, too, can prevail over their challenges. You might have tips or strategies to help them do so.

On a different level, as an Activist, you may want to make a difference, with that desire growing out of your values. You believe motivating others to do better is the right thing to do. Your ethics and morals guide your activism and your purpose. You know something needs to be fixed, and you sense you are a person who can get the ball rolling.

Possibly you feel internally pushed to make a difference. You may or may not possess certainty about what you are meant to do or how, but something compels you to contribute. As a spiritual person, you believe you have a life purpose—you feel your soul came into this world in this lifetime to do something specific. It's your job as a human being to complete that task. You know what you need to do—or you think you do—and are ready to do it. You believe something—a universal force—urges you to make a difference, and it's your responsibility to heed the calling and become a Transformer.

Whether you see your purpose clearly or it remains out of focus, a book can help you achieve it. However, clarity of purpose drives the writing of your book. Plus, as a change agent, you need to share your purpose in a way that others understand.

Choose Your Purpose

You can identify your purpose on any of the levels mentioned above. Or you can stop waiting for your purpose to reveal itself to you and choose one. You don't even have to categorize your desire to effect change as a calling, movement, or cause. Just get clear about the type of change you want to inspire and why.

It's that simple.

You can decide, "It is my purpose to help people love themselves. I see how my own lack of self-love impacted my health, happiness, and success and how learning to love myself unconditionally made me healthier, happier, more successful, and able to love and be loved. I've noticed how many people—young and old—struggle simply because they don't love themselves. So, I want to write a book that shares my story and offers tips and strategies that increase readers' ability to love themselves." Awesome!

Or you might decide, "It is my purpose to make a positive difference in the field of immigrant rights. I've known many undocumented immigrants who contribute greatly to my community or who arrived in the United States as children—like my best friend. I want to support efforts to expand and stand up for their civil liberties and combat discrimination against them. I'm ready to devote my life to immigrant rights. It's an important cause that hits close to home and affects so many people around the world. I'm going to begin my efforts by writing a book." Perfect!

Here are a few ways to choose your purpose and tie a change-inspiring book to it:

- Identify your passions. Choose one as the focus of your book.
- Determine the unique gifts you have. (Your friends, family, and coworkers probably compliment you on these regularly.) If you can do something well—and others don't have that ability—focus your book on sharing that gift.
- Find what excites or upsets you. Write about that.

Eight Questions about Your Purpose

Take a moment to examine what you already know about your purpose by answering the following questions. You can explore your responses in a journal.

- Was there a pivotal event that caused me to develop a sense of purpose?
- When did I decide I wanted to inspire change?
- Why did I decide I wanted to inspire change?
- Do I have one or many ways to make an impact in the world?
- What is my greatest passion?
- What matters to me the most?
- Who would I most like to impact?
- If I had unlimited resources and could use them to change the world, what would I do?

Based on your answers to the above questions, clearly state your purpose. For additional insights, you can use meditation, journaling, and visualizing.

Meditation: You can choose from many types of meditation, but I suggest an intentional one—a period when you focus your mind on finding an answer to a question. Find a quiet place where you won't be disturbed, close your eyes, and pay attention to your breathing for a few moments. In this state, pose a question to yourself, like: "Why do I want to effect change?" "Why do I want to write a book?" "What's my purpose?" or "How do I want to be of service?" Then listen for an answer—a thought that shows up and refuses to go away or elicits strong emotions. If your mind strays, bring it back to the question by asking it again. Take as long as you like for this meditation, and if necessary, repeat it daily until you receive an answer. And pay attention—the answer may show up as a "sign" of some sort.

Journaling: Have a journal nearby when you do the meditation above. Then, immediately after completing your reflection, jot down the answers you received during meditation. Take time to explore them further.

If you don't want to meditate, pose the suggested meditation questions to yourself in your journal; compose your responses in the blank pages. Give yourself at least thirty minutes for this exercise. If you don't arrive at some conclusion by the end of that time, ask yourself the same questions again and record your additional responses each day. Each time you will get closer to the truth.

Visualization: A visualization is a form of meditation that involves painting a picture in your mind. Using your imagination in this way provides a powerful way to mentally access or seed information. Here's a visualization you can use to uncover your purpose.

Take a few deep breaths. Imagine yourself causing positive change. Allow your mind to take you where it will as you see and feel what it would be like to successfully create transformation. Pay attention to who you interact with, what actions you take, or how you create change. Notice what feels good and what doesn't, what excites you or causes resistance, and what makes your body feel loose and open or tight and closed. Positive emotional and physical responses lead directly to your purpose.

If you don't feel emotions as you visualize, trust what seem like your purest thoughts about purpose. These are the ones untainted by past experiences, things you've been taught, or external belief systems. Such thoughts may resound loudly in your head, or they may show up as whispers but feel accurate and relevant to the moment. They won't be based on what you think you should do or what others have told you to do. Nor will they have their foundation in past experiences that left you with fears or negativity. These thoughts will excite, inspire, and motivate you and lead to your purpose.

If you continue to struggle with the idea of purpose or how to clarify and articulate yours, it's likely your negative thoughts and limiting beliefs are influencing your ability to decide on a purpose. Although they may leave you feeling confused and unworthy, these feelings, thoughts, and beliefs are not the truth. Dig deep inside to find the initial inspiration that led you to consider becoming a change agent or writing a transformational book. That's where you'll find your purpose.

You set out to serve; therein lies the seed of your purpose. You can do so in any number of ways, including by writing a book.

Now, fill in the blank in this sentence with what you hope to accomplish: *It is my purpose to* _____. For example, you might write, *It is my purpose to improve immigrant rights.* Here are a few other examples: *It is my purpose to increase humanity's self-love quotient. It is my purpose to eradicate white supremacy. It is my purpose to help people attract abundance. It is my purpose to reduce school shootings. It is my purpose to teach people how to be happier. It is my purpose to create conscious leaders.*

Your Mission Statement

With your purpose clarified, let's consider *what* you will achieve by fulfilling it. Your *purpose* is your reason for creating change; your *mission* is the goal that fulfills your purpose. Therefore, your mission flows out of your purpose, and your book provides a way to accomplish it.

A mission, like a goal, needs a clear result. Without clarity on the result, it's hard to know if or when you have achieved it. Additionally, you want your audience to recognize the desired outcome and the benefits they will receive from it. This information influences them to read your book or agree to change.

Consider the results you are striving to achieve. Do you want to accomplish any or all of the following:

- Leave a legacy for your children or the world?
- Help someone in particular, or a certain type of person?
- Assist a large group of people?
- Enroll X number of people in your cause?
- Increase awareness of a problem and propose solutions?

Imagine that you want to help foster parents and foster children. Your purpose—your reason for instigating change—might be: *I grew up in the foster care system. I was not supported in developing aspirations or the means to achieve them. I had no idea how to succeed in life and had to learn this on my own. Therefore, I want to give back and teach foster parents what I now know, and in this way, help foster children succeed in life.*

Your mission—what you hope to achieve with your book about foster parents—might be expressed in a statement that sounds a lot like your purpose statement: *It's my mission to help foster children succeed at life.*

That's a start. Let's expand on it, though. How will you know you've accomplished your mission—that you've created the result you desire? You might decide: *To achieve my mission, I need to prove that the number of foster children who enter college, graduate, and land jobs in their chosen career is increasing year over year.*

You've identified your purpose and mission. Now it's time to create a *mission statement*. You will use this statement as you ask people to join your movement. They will resonate with your personal reasons for taking up a cause as much as they will with their own. Beyond that, you must have a definitive goal in mind that others can buy into.

Mission statements are a tried-and-true staple of successful businesses and organizations. A focused mission has been proven to help employees, investors, and customers know what the company does and why. Many authors offer a mission statement on their websites and in marketing materials for the same reason. Plus, the mission statement guides their book writing.

As you write your mission statement, remember that your Big Why provides the emotional connection to your mission. When you express that, your audience unites with your purpose and with you on a similar emotional level. If they feel aligned with your mission, they buy your book and take the actions it recommends.

How to Craft a Mission Statement

Use the following formula to craft your mission statement:

Audience + Service = Transformation. Include the following elements:

1. Who you help—your *audience*
2. What you help your audience do—your *service*
3. The result they achieve—the *transformation*

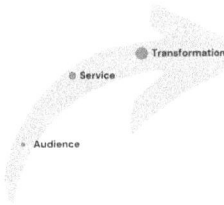

Your *audience* consists of anyone interested in the change you want to inspire. These people can implement the change or take it on for themselves. For instance, your audience might be single mothers, people who lost a relative or friend to COVID-19, gun owners, those suffering from heartbreak, people with Lyme disease, CEOs, environmentalists, veterans, or people who practice Transcendental Meditation. The more specifically you can identify your audience, the better—such as single mothers who have no life balance, people who have suffered from Lyme disease for more than five years, parents of children who died of COVID-19, or city officials who can impact what is done with empty spaces.

There are also *adjacent audiences*—readers who are related to your primary audience. For instance, you might attract doctors and parents to a mission that involves a change in the treatment of long-term Lyme disease. Craft your book's mission statement around your primary audience, but keep the others in mind.

Let's return to the previous example about improving the lives of foster children in the U.S. Your audience would consist primarily of foster parents and officials in the child welfare system. You might enlist the help of former foster children and parents of children who were placed in the foster care system as well, which would make them adjacent audiences. Ultimately, you help foster children, but you do so by being of *service* to the *audience* that will read your book and impact the lives of the children.

Your audience has the power to make a difference if they act based upon your recommendations. You are of *service* to your audience by proposing changes your audience can make to improve some condition or situation. In the foster parent example above, you serve your audience by giving them what they need to impact the lives of those *they* serve. That's the *transformation* you create—improving foster parents' ability to help their foster children succeed in life.

Write a sentence that answers the question "What do you do?" and includes the three elements mentioned earlier: your audience, how you serve that audience, and the transformation you help them achieve. For instance, *I help foster parents* (the audience) *learn how to raise children's aspirations, self-esteem, and self-confidence* (the service) *so the children succeed in life* (the transformation).

When you get clear about your mission and how you will know when you have completed it, you can determine if you've authored change. Add to your mission statement a sentence that clearly identifies the result you desire. For instance, you might say: *It is my intention to increase the number of foster children who attend college and successfully enter the workforce by 50 percent in five years.*

Your mission statement would then read like this: *I help foster parents learn how to raise children's aspirations, self-esteem, and self-confidence so the children succeed in life. I intend to increase the number of foster children who attend college and successfully enter the workforce by 50 percent in five years.*

Let's look at a different example. Suppose your purpose and mission revolve around helping people heal heartbreak related to a failed long-term relationship. In that case, your *audience* might include men and women struggling to get over a divorce or breakup after three years or more in a relationship. You could narrow this audience further by addressing only heartbroken women. Adjacent audiences might include family members and friends of those who are heartbroken, as well as therapists, coaches, and psychologists who deal with heartbreak. You would then be of *service* to women who are heartbroken and all those who can support them through the healing process. Your *transformation* would be the healing of women's heartbreak.

Your intention might be *to help women get over heartbreak faster and come out of the experience stronger and more able to create a new long-term loving relationship.*

With this example, your mission statement could read like this: *I help heartbroken women* (audience) *learn how to heal, regain their personal power and confidence, and utilize relationship tools* (the service) *so they are able to create new, fulfilling, joyous, loving, and lasting relationships* (the transformation). *I intend to help women get over heartbreak faster and come out of the experience stronger and more able to create a new long-term loving relationship.*

How a Book Fits into Your Mission

It's also imperative to consider how writing a book fits into your mission. Why do you want to write a transformational book? After all, you may consider yourself a change agent rather than a writer. As such, you could choose from a variety of other ways to further your cause. Knowing why you have chosen the route of authorship strengthens your commitment to the book and writing it.

If you are a writer, it may seem logical to put your change efforts into a book. Still, a clearly identified mission for writing that book increases your commitment to publishing it. When you know who your audience is and why they need this book now—not later—and how you can serve them, you feel motivated to create transformation for them. Your emotional connection to your Big Why for writing the book increases the urgency you feel to complete the project and, as a result, keeps you writing consistently.

I've encountered many aspiring transformational authors who, when asked, cannot tell me how their audience will be impacted by their books. These writers typically come to me when they feel stuck and aren't writing consistently. When they identify their readers' urgent need for their book, they feel motivated to write. Sometimes, they have to recall a time when they needed a book like the one they plan to write or think about the impact it will have on their audience if they do *not* write the book.

Indeed, there are people out there who need your book. They want you to be of service to them. They seek transformation. Remember that as you write your book's mission statement.

Answer these questions: *Why do I feel compelled to write a book? Why do I think a book will help me fulfill my mission?* Following our previous example, if your book is about how foster parents can help foster children succeed in life, you might write: *I feel compelled to write this book first, because I want to help foster children succeed in life, and second, because becoming an author will help me be perceived as an expert, which in turn will give me authority, so I will have increased influence to make a difference with foster parents. The book also provides me with a way to share what I know with foster parents all over the country. To date, I've only shared with them in small groups or during one-on-one conversations.*

If you want to help women heal quickly from heartbreak and develop the ability to create new, lasting relationships, you might say, *I feel compelled to write this book because too many women who experience heartbreak remain single when they get stuck in the past and can't envision—let alone create—a new long-term relationship. Yet they deserve to experience love—sooner rather than later. The book will allow me to serve heartbroken women around the world. Additionally, it will lead readers to my coaching practice, which in turn will allow me to help heartbroken women in private or group settings.*

Now you have a personal mission statement and a clear understanding of how writing your book helps you accomplish it. It's time to move on to writing your book's mission statement, which arises from your personal mission statement.

Your Book's Mission Statement

Your book will have more impact in the world if its message is concise and quickly understood by those whose support you seek. Therefore, it needs a mission statement of its own. However, this statement should align with your personal mission. After all, you are writing the book to help you achieve that goal, and you will express your mission in the book's pages. Also, your book's clear mission statement guides your writing process and shines through all aspects of the book—including its cover, chapters, and marketing—and inspires people to read it and take action. You will refer to it when you speak to an audience of any size, even if it's just one person standing in line with you in the checkout aisle who asks what your book is about.

The book's mission statement needs to be less about you and more about its benefits—the results the book promises its readers will achieve. When a potential reader asks, "What is your book about?" they want to know, "What's in it for me?" In other words, they are wondering, "What value does the book hold for me specifically? How will I benefit from reading it?" Your book's mission statement answers those questions.

You may have heard the common writing advice to "know your reader" and "write for your reader." You've already identified an audience, a specific target group to serve. Become knowledgeable, if you aren't already, about your audience's desires, problems, questions, challenges, and what motivates them to act. Use this information to craft your book's mission statement (and to write your book).

Let's take the previous work you've done and extrapolate your book's mission statement. For instance, recall the mission statement related to foster parenting, which was written using a three-part formula (audience + service = transformation). It reads: *I help foster parents learn how to raise children's aspirations, self-esteem, and self-confidence, so the children succeed in life. It is my intention to increase the number of foster children who attend college and successfully enter the workforce by 50 percent in five years.*

Now use the same three-part formula—tweaked a bit—to create your book's mission statement. You might articulate it this way: *My book teaches foster parents* (the audience) *how to raise children's aspirations, self-esteem, and self-confidence* (the service) *so they succeed at life* (the transformation). Notice how this statement identifies the audience—foster parents. And it offers specific information on the benefits readers will achieve—the ability to help foster children succeed in life.

However, this statement does not yet include information about *how* the author will accomplish these results—the service provided. That's what marketers call a unique selling proposition (USP), and you need it to complete your book's mission statement. Your *how* might be a series of steps, a particular methodology, a framework, or suggested habits, mindsets, or strategies.

With this final element added, the mission statement for the book about raising foster children might read like this: *My book teaches foster parents* (the audience) *a step-by-step process* (how) *to raise children's aspirations, self-esteem, and self-confidence* (the service) *so they succeed at life* (the transformation).

The more specific you can get about your USP, the better. Answer the following four questions as another way to craft your book's mission statement and add more detail:

1. **Who** (the audience) do I want to help, or who am I writing this book for? Be specific about your readers. (Example: *My book will help the approximately 370,000 children in foster care in the United States by addressing those who work in the field of child welfare or are foster parents.*)
2. **Why** (the meaningful reason) would these people take up your cause or be interested in the transformation you promise? (Example: *They care for foster children, are concerned for their welfare, and want to see them succeed. However, currently, only 71 percent of foster children in the U.S. receive a high school diploma by age nineteen; only 55 percent of former foster youth attend college; and of that group, only 8 percent graduate.*)

3. ***What*** (the transformation) benefits does your book provide to the reader, or what do you promise to help them accomplish? (Example: *I have a strategy that when applied by parents in a family where foster children are struggling, dramatically improves the children's self-esteem, increases their ability to create a powerful dream or vision, and helps them take steps to build a successful future.*)

4. ***How*** (your unique solution or strategy) will your book help these potential readers achieve the result you mentioned in #2? How will you help them change? (Example: *It will provide a step-by-step system of daily communication, planning, brainstorming, action steps, visualization, and result tracking that foster parents can use to help foster children create a goal for the future, become confident in their ability to achieve it, and take concrete and consistent action to make that future a reality.*)

Now write your book's mission statement using the answers to the above questions. Don't be afraid to rewrite or reorder the answers. You want to create a compelling and concise mission statement. For instance: *Currently, only 71 percent of foster children in the U.S. receive a high school diploma by age nineteen; only 55 percent of former foster youth attend college; and of that group, only 8 percent graduate. My book will help the approximately 370,000 children in foster care in the United States by providing foster parents with a step-by-step system of daily communication, planning, brainstorming, action steps, visualization, and result tracking that will help them support their foster children in creating goals for the future, becoming confident in their ability to achieve them, and taking concrete and consistent action to make that future a reality.*

Your book's mission statement becomes its GPS. It helps you navigate the writing of the manuscript and ensures that every page guides your reader toward the benefits—the transformation—you promised and the achievement of your mission.

Fulfilling Your Purpose and Achieving Your Mission

How do you fulfill your purpose? By accomplishing your mission. You do that in part by publishing a book. How do you know if your book has accomplished its mission? It lands in the hands of readers and creates the transformation you intended.

To help you to discover your next steps toward fulfilling your purpose and to uncover the details that allow you to complete your mission, consider:

- **How many books you need to write.** Sometimes it takes more than one book to fulfill your purpose or complete your mission. Are there other books you might write after this one that support your purpose and mission? Brainstorm the subjects of other possible books and determine the order in which you would release them to best achieve the transformation you want to inspire.
- **What else you need to do.** Besides writing a book, what do you need to do to fulfill your purpose and accomplish your mission? Of course, you need to publish the book. Maybe you also need a website or a blog on which you post consistently. Would a podcast or speaking engagements help? Do you need to focus on building an email list and doing email marketing—or would a direct marketing campaign help more? You may need to create an event, start an online group, develop a meme, or create a Facebook page and profile. (You will learn more about these options in Part 2.)
- **How many books you hope to sell.** Does having a bestselling book, one that sells more copies than the competition, help you succeed? Many authors and change agents strive to have significant reach with their message; they want to get as many books as possible into the hands of their target audiences. You may relate to that goal, or

book sales may have nothing to do with fulfilling your purpose or achieving your mission. You may only want to enact change in a small niche. If you see the transformation happening with that small audience, you'll feel successful even if you've only sold two hundred copies.

- **What achieving your mission means.** Quantify the results that equate to success. What do you need to achieve to feel you have accomplished your mission? Do you intend to reach two thousand foster parents during the first year after the release of your book and see college acceptance of foster children increase by 50 percent in the next five years? Do you want to help one thousand heartbroken women heal and find love in the first two years after your book hits the market?
- **How fulfilling your purpose looks or feels.** When your life nears its end, how will you know you fulfilled your purpose? Will you feel satisfied with the change you inspired; or will you see and experience the transformation you motivated? Maybe you will have a sense of satisfaction, success, or abundance. Possibly you will encounter people who will tell you that your work—and your book—made a difference in their lives.

Take a moment to visualize your purpose fulfilled. Write down the details you see with your mind's eye in your journal; or decide on the criteria that indicate success. List the results you want to achieve—for yourself and the reader. If your nonfiction how-to book is meant to inspire more urban micro-farming across the world, you might write: *My book about urban micro-farming continues to be a bestseller twenty years after its release, which means it has landed in the hands of thousands of people. I see the effects of the book's success in the world. It has inspired visible change in cities around the world and increased the number of micro-farms by five hundred in the first ten years after its release. Today, urban dwellers enjoy more beautiful cities and amazingly fresh and healthy food grown locally.*

Congratulations! You have clarified your purpose and your mission. Your mission statement and your book's mission statement will both serve you well and move you toward successfully authoring change. Now, you are ready to move on to the next step—understanding change. To author change, you must possess the ability to influence readers to do something differently. Let's look at how people change and how you can inspire your readers to act in ways that improve their lives or the world.

PART ONE
HOW TO EMBODY CHANGE

3
UNDERSTAND CHANGE

"To inspire change, you must understand it. Those who want to create transformation have an intimate relationship with change and know what makes someone do things differently or take a stand. That knowledge helps them inspire change and motivate people to action. It helps them ignite a movement and keep it burning and step into the role of change agent. The knowledge of how people adapt fosters an understanding of how to create change on a larger scale."

— MAHATMA GANDHI

Books that can change the world must compel readers page by page to initiate and pursue a change process. The change may be as minor as waking up earlier, such as Hal Elrod's *The Miracle Morning*, or as large as doing something that potentially could save the planet, like *Climate of Hope* by Michael Bloomberg and Carl Pope. To get people to do something different, you must understand what makes them change and use that knowledge as you write your book. Additionally, you need to be intimate with change—you need to have experienced transformation, know how you respond to change, or be in the process of change. Then your personal experiences and understanding inform the content of your book and enhance your ability to motivate change in readers' lives.

Let's start our discussion of change with five foundational principles. First, *change is an active process, while transformation is a state* of having thoroughly morphed into something else. *The act of change—* or taking action toward a desired change—*causes and results in transformation.*

State of Transformation

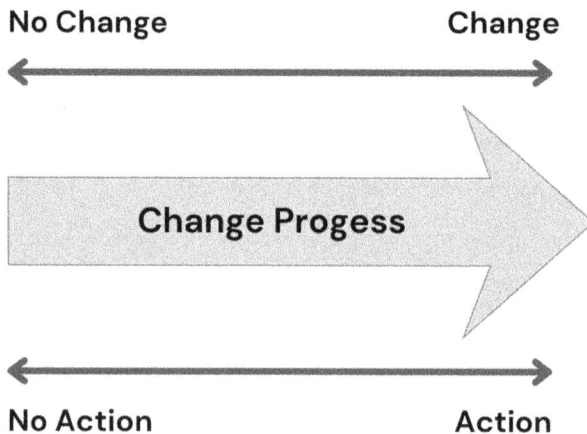

No Change **Change**

← →

Change Progess

← →

No Action **Action**

Second, *change is ongoing and happening now*—whether you know it or not, and whether you like or dislike it. As Heraclitus said, "The only thing that is constant is change." Consider the fact that the political climate can change in a moment, the stock market can crash in a day, and the weather changes hour by hour. Also, the lining of your stomach renews itself every few days, and your epidermis reju-venates every two to four weeks. Likewise, your emotions can change from happy to sad in an instant, and your energy can go up or down simply by encountering another human being or digesting your most recent meal.

Third, *many of us resist change.* According to a study conducted by Mount Eliza Business School, over 70 percent of change initiatives fail because of people's resistance. Other studies reveal that 91 percent of patients who underwent heart bypass surgery resisted adjusting their lifestyle—although not doing so could shorten their life expectancy. Even when people have dreams and goals, if achieving them requires change, they too often do what's easiest and safest—they stay the same. Obviously, resistance poses a challenge for an aspiring Author of Change. The more your readers resist change, the harder it becomes for you, the writer, to lead them toward transformation.

Fourth, *even though few people like to change, most accept—even embrace—the big life changes*, like getting married, changing jobs, and adopting new technologies. That means *people can and do change.*

Fifth, *you can't force anyone to change*, and angrily insisting on change is a broken strategy. If you attempt either of these things, your atti-tude and energy will be met with higher levels of resistance from your audience. And as Carl Jung contended, "What you resist not only persists but will grow in size."

Clearly, getting people to join your cause, movement, or mission requires a deep understanding of human beings and what makes them want to take a stand, contribute, or do something different. That fact remains the same no matter if you want to create more peace and happiness or positive climate change. It is true whether you want to move people to become meditators, intuitive leaders, or conscious parents. And you will still need this understanding if you desire your readers to try automatic writing, a healing diet, or a nonpartisan approach to politics. But don't dismay. You can author change.

Tony Robbins, personal development speaker and author of *Unlimited Power*, claims change happens the moment someone makes "a new, congruent, and committed decision" and follows it with "massive action." In this chapter, you will find strategies to help your readers *decide* to do something different and take bold *action*. You will know your book has guided them to a decision aligned with who they want to be when they take lasting and consistent steps toward transformation for themselves, others, or the greater good.

Let's look at how to make that happen—first in yourself and then in others.

Understanding Your Relationship to Change

To help your readers embrace change, you must do the same. You may believe you already do, but a closer examination of how you deal with change may reveal that, like most people, you resist it in certain situations. In subsequent chapters, you also might discover the need to make changes yourself in order to successfully author change. If you resist changing, you will struggle to produce a book that makes a difference—even though that is your goal.

However, if you decide to *be* an Author of Change—to show up now as a person who writes books that impact lives, families, communities, businesses, or the world—you will act in a manner congruent with that identity. You will write a book that makes a difference. So, decide that you already are an Author of Change even if you haven't yet written or published the book. Next, do what is necessary to write a book that profoundly impacts those who read it.

Your initial task as an Author of Change involves coupling your new identity with a deep understanding of how you influence yourself to do new things—how you *author change in your own life*. Your insights inform your efforts to *author change in your readers' lives or in the world at large.* To gain that understanding, examine your relationship to change in the following four ways.

1. **Examine your past relationship to change.**

First, look backward. How have you previously felt about change? When have you changed? Knowing how or why you have successfully changed allows you to repeat that process—and tell others how you did it.

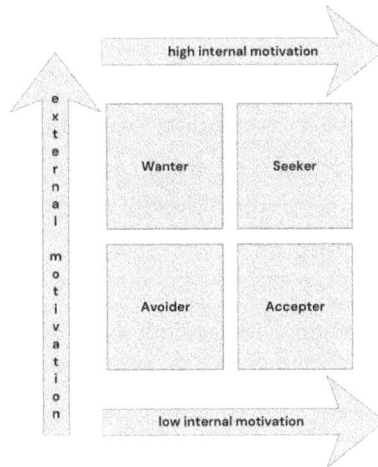

The graphic above demonstrates the correlation between internal and external motivation on your desire to change. The terms Avoider, Accepter, Wanter, and Seeker describe your identity in relationship to desiring change or needing to be forced to change. The higher the external motivation to do something differently, the stronger the likelihood that you will change even if you tend to avoid change, or want change but tend not to accept or seek it. However, the higher your internal motivation, the greater the chances you will move from avoiding change to accepting change and then actually wanting and seeking transformation.

Some people are good at avoiding change. Low internal motivation causes these "Avoiders" to dodge and run from the external factors that might force them to change. Most people wait for something external to force change upon them or motivate change and then adapt as necessary. They are the "Accepters."

Other people want change but struggle to act on their desire. These "Wanters" need increased amounts of internal or external motivation to create change. Then there are those who thrive on change and actively seek it out. These change "Seekers" rarely need external motivation but welcome it. For them, the desire for change comes from within.

In the past, have you been an avoider, accepter, wanter, or seeker? Think of situations in which you were each of these. Then, in your journal, explore why you found yourself in those roles. You might find these prompts helpful:

- I was an avoider when... The reason I was an avoider is...
- I was an accepter when... I was an accepter because...
- I was a wanter when... The reason I was a wanter is...
- I was a seeker when... I was a seeker because...

2. Assess where you are now in the change process.

It's common to get stuck at different stages of change. Understanding where you are now on the Stages of Change Model created by James O. Prochaska and Carlo DiClemente helps you move to the next stage. You can complete this exercise with authorship in mind: *Where are you in the process of authoring change?*

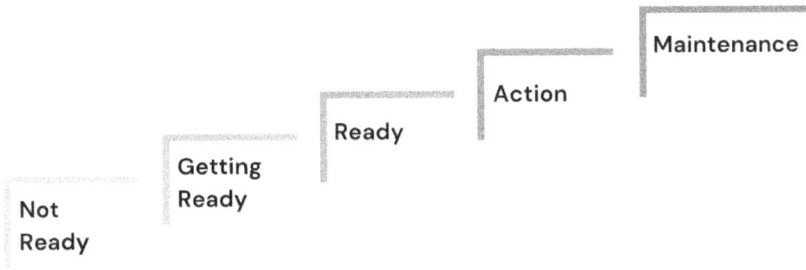

If you are in or tend to linger in the Not Ready (*Precontemplation*) stage, you have no intention of changing in the next six months. You may be uninformed or underinformed about the consequences of your behavior, or you may have failed at change in the past; that lack of information or failure to change now colors your sense of being ready and able to change in the present. Some may see you as resistant, unmotivated, or unready for help. In your journal, complete this sentence: *I am in the precontemplation stage in the following areas of my journey to authoring change...* Then explore why you are in that stage.

When you enter (or remain stuck in) the Getting Ready (*Contemplation*) stage, you seriously think about changing at some point in the next six months. You may be aware of the pros and cons related to change, but you feel ambivalent and continue to weigh the costs and benefits. People who get stuck in this stage often characterize themselves as "overthinkers" and stay in their heads rather than taking bold action. In your journal, complete this sentence: *I am in the contemplation stage in the following areas of my journey to authoring change...* Then explore why you are in that stage.

If you are in the Ready (*Preparation*) stage, you plan to act in the next month. You may have an action plan and feel almost ready to take that step. Complete this prompt in your journal: *I am in the preparation stage in the following areas of my journey to authoring change...* Also explore why you are in that stage.

In the *Action* stage, you have taken observable—and possibly consistent, if not yet habitual—action toward transformation in the last six months. In your journal, complete this sentence: *I am in the action stage in the following areas of my journey to authoring change...* Explore why you are in the Action stage.

Last, if you are in the *Maintenance* stage, you've made specific outward modifications in your lifestyle and are working to keep up your habits. In your journal, complete this sentence: *I am in the maintenance stage in the following areas of my journey to authoring change...* Then, explore how you can tackle new change that will allow you to go to the next level.

You are likely in different stages depending on the activities necessary to write and publish a book. Similarly, if you apply this framework to other life arenas, you will find yourself at different stages when it comes to health, work, finances, or relationships.

Your Change Assessment

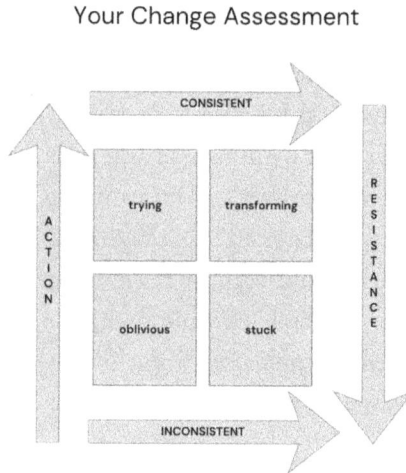

Let's look at the change process in another way. The graphic above helps you determine where you are on the journey to change—whether you are oblivious to the need for change, stuck and unable to change, trying to change (maybe with few results), or transforming (experiencing the process of change). The lower your degree of resistance, the more likely you are to take action that leads to transformation. The more actions you take to create change, the greater the chances that you achieve transformation. The degree of *consistent* action taken also determines if you continue the process of change until you experience transformation. Inconsistent action keeps you stuck or trying—although even the action of becoming aware that you need to change moves you forward (toward the state of knowing you are either stuck or trying to change). Consistent action with low resistance moves you quickly from being stuck or trying to change to transformation.

You might be *oblivious* to the need to change—you think you can simply sit down and write a book that will change the world, and there's nothing more to it; you don't realize that you yourself need to change. Maybe you need to become a writer by creating a daily writing habit or an influencer by posting on social media to build an audience for your movement. Perhaps you are *stuck*—you realize you need to begin building a community around your movement and write consistently but feel overwhelmed and unable to act. Or you might be *trying* to change—you've started on your manuscript and set up social media accounts for your cause but aren't taking consistent action. Perhaps you are in the process of *transforming*—you regularly write and work to build community but know you still need to change in a variety of other ways if you want to successfully author change.

Take a moment to journal your responses to the following sentence completion exercise. Use writing and publishing your book as the focus of the exercise.

- *I am oblivious to the need to change to become an author. My "blind spots" are:* _____ (Note: Being oblivious means you don't know you need to change. As such, this constitutes a blind spot, and it may feel difficult to complete this prompt. If so, ask friends, family, or other writers for input—or read subsequent chapters to discover required changes. You also might know how you need to change but haven't admitted that fact to yourself; now is the time to do so.)

- *To become an Author of Change, I know I need to change but feel unable to get started in the following areas: _____. What keeps me stuck is _____.*
- *To become an Author of Change, I'm trying to change in the following ways: _____. What I am doing to change is_____. Where I am struggling to change is_____.*
- *To become an Author of Change, I am transforming in the following ways: _____. What has helped me change and transform is_____.*

3. Determine how you need to change now.

The previous assessments provide an understanding of your relationship with change and where you are in the process—at least when it comes to authorship. Review your position on the three frameworks (the Stages of Change Model, Your Relationship to Change, and Your Change Assessment). Then, consider why you fall into those positions and what you need to do to move closer to embracing change—especially as it relates to becoming an author. Specifically, note any changes you are now aware you need to make to become an Author of Change. (If you found any part of this exercise difficult, read the next chapter and then come back to complete it.)

With your mission in mind, in your journal, record everything about the changes you previously made—what was easy or hard, the length of time it took you to change, what prompted the change, who helped you change, and what beliefs, feelings, mindsets, experiences, or events caused you to change. Also, journal about how you still need to change and the impact of changing—on yourself, others, or a larger community.

Review what you have written and highlight any new insights into your relationship with change. Make a note of any stories related to change you could share both in your book and when speaking to audiences, appearing on podcasts, posting on social media, and writing blog posts and email letters.

4. Apply what you learned to writing your book.

Your ability to share your struggles and successes makes you more relatable to your audience. Plus, when you express your previous challenges and how you overcame them, your readers develop an increased belief that they, too, can move past their resistance. They will trust you to show them how. However, for that trust to develop, you must share your understanding of the change process with readers.

The exploration you have completed has deepened your understanding of what it previously took for you to change, which will prove helpful as you choose to take on new attitudes, behaviors, and activities related to authorship. For now, though, apply that knowledge to how your readers react to change and decide to do things differently. Then, use this understanding to write a book that moves them to action.

Understanding Your Readers' Relationship to Change

Just like you, your readers are at one stage or another on the change frameworks previously shared. Therefore, how you motivate them to change largely depends upon where they are on these models. That's why it's essential for you to understand how your readers go through the process of change.

In Chapter 2, you identified your audience. These are your "ideal readers," the people you hope will purchase your book and join your movement. It's imperative to know exactly to whom you are speaking when you write. Only then can you know how to help, inspire, or motivate them. So, if you are still unclear about your audience specifics, take time to create an "ideal reader" profile in your journal. Include information on your readers' goals, values, interests, hobbies, hangouts, demographics, aspirations, challenges, emotional issues, negative thoughts and objections (to change), questions, and problems. Consider what they want and what they need. You can even give this ideal reader a name if you like. For example, *Nancy is a 45-year-old professional who owns a virtual coaching business. She lives in Batavia, Illinois, where she and her husband own a house. She has two elementary school-aged children and has been married fifteen years. She earns $100,000 per year. In her free time, she goes horseback riding, reads, and goes to the gym. Her highest values are family, contribution, and mental and physical health. Her most significant challenges are finding time to grow her business and improve her marriage. What she really wants is more time. But what she needs is to become more productive, learn to say "no" to volunteer opportunities, and stick to her schedule.*

You can also describe how your reader feels about and deals with change. To do this, again review the frameworks and complete the exercises previously shared in this chapter—this time with your reader in mind. Make a note of where your readers fall on the Stages of Change, Your Relationship to Change, and Your Change Assessment frameworks. Then, complete the journal exercise above as if you are your "ideal reader." Your answers will provide insight into how to help your readers change.

For instance, are your readers stuck at one point in the change process, like preparation? If so, how might you get them to take a new action step? What helped you make that move? Are they oblivious to the need to change? If so, how will you make them aware of what lies in their blind spot? What made you aware of the need to change?

How you motivate your readers to change largely depends upon your understanding of their perspective on and behavior related to change. Of course, authoring change also relies on your knowledge of how you and all people change, as well as your ability to utilize that knowledge when writing your book.

How to Move Your Reader Toward Transformation

Five primary strategies help move people toward transformation. Implementing one or more of these as you write your book increases your readers' likelihood of achieving transformation.

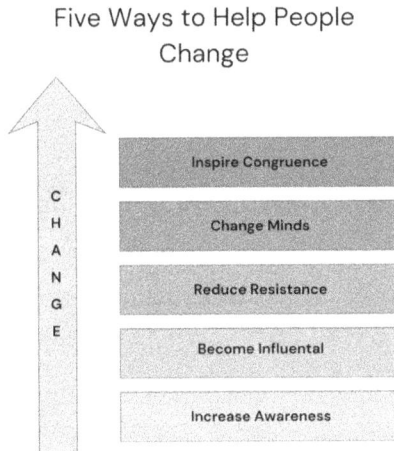

Five Ways to Help People
Change

Inspire Congruence

Change Minds

Reduce Resistance

Become Influental

Increase Awareness

1. **Increase Awareness**

Some people don't realize they need to change. (Remember your blind spot?) If your audience is oblivious to this fact, first, increase their awareness level. Point out what's lacking in their situation or the world and how change provides benefit. If they are already aware, increase their degree of awareness. The more conscious your readers become of an issue and their options for addressing it—or the pain or loss they will experience by not addressing it—the more likely it is they will decide to set change in motion. As Robbins says, "It is in your moments of decision that your destiny is shaped. A real decision is measured by the fact that you've taken a new action. If there's no action, you haven't truly decided."

Increase your readers' awareness level with the following four strategies:

Use Powerful Questions—Daniel Pink, the author of *Drive: The Surprising Truth About What Motivates Us*, claims utilizing questions provides a critical tool for influencing behavior because questions elicit active responses and thought processes. Here's a good example: During the 1980 U.S. presidential election, President Ronald Raegan asked, "Are you better off than you were four years ago?" That same question was used repeatedly in the 2024 U.S. presidential election. Questions make people aware of their own reasons for doing something and increase their desire to act.

T. Harv Eker, the author of *Secrets of the Millionaire Mind*, often asks his audience questions with two positive choices—both the same, such as "Good or good?" "True or true?" This makes people aware that they agree with him. For example, I could say or write: "Learning to author change helps you have a global impact. Yes or yes?"

Asking your readers rhetorical questions increases awareness, too. For example: "Wouldn't you like to know you've made the world a safer place for your children?" or "It would be amazing to have changed the culture of your company even a little bit, right?"

You can also raise your audience's level of awareness by asking thought-provoking questions like:

"What do you want?"

"Is your approach working?"

"What will your life look like in three years if nothing changes?"

"How would you like your future to look? Will it look like that if you keep doing what you've been doing?"

"What stops you from taking new action?"

"What would become possible if you changed?"

These queries make your readers aware of their struggles and aspirations, as well as their desire to bridge the gap between where they are now and where they want to be. The inquiry process avoids directly asking your audience to change, which can cause resistance, and instead allows them to come to their own decision to do so.

Stir the Pot—To get people to make a purchase, marketers stoke the audience's unhappiness or point out their pain points. Called "stirring the pot," this strategy makes the audience aware of their level of dissatisfaction or discomfort. As a result, they decide to take action that provides relief.

Suppose you are working on a book about how to afford retirement. You might employ this strategy by writing: "You imagined you'd have achieved a greater level of success by now, and with it, financial security. Instead, the tiny bit of money you've managed to stash away for retirement isn't enough to allow you to retire...ever."

Your readers will relate to your description of their experience and know you understand their situation. Naturally, this piques their curiosity about how you can help them decrease their clear and present discomfort.

Of course, you don't want to leave readers feeling uncomfortable. So, after stirring the pot, shift their focus from struggle to aspiration—what they want, not what they don't want. You might ask, "What would it be like if you had more than enough money in the bank to retire? What would become possible?" Help them see a vision for a compelling future and believe they can achieve it. Then, they'll become aware that change is possible.

At this point, you might share your strategy for creating personal change—one thing the reader can do to begin the process of transformation. For example, in *Do One Thing,* Sue Hadfield suggests busy professionals find greater satisfaction by altering one aspect of their personal life.

Tell Stories—Stories provide an important transformational tool. Increase your readers' awareness and motivation by sharing the story of your own transformation, which you uncovered earlier in this chapter. Or share those of others creating change personally, professionally, or globally.

Craft your stories so the audience shares in your experience. For example, if you describe your first kiss, every member in your audience naturally sees and experiences their first kiss as if it was happening in the moment. Each story you share needs to paint a beautiful picture of the future you hope to create with your readers so they see and experience themselves in that mind movie.

Stories are accessible and enormously powerful because they create mental images, memory recall, and emotions. In addition, effective stories provide a link between struggle and success. For instance, if you tell your readers a story about how you turned your manufacturing company into a conscious business model, they see the possibility of accomplishing that transformation.

Stories also help you avoid telling people they are wrong, bad, or should do things differently. No one responds well to that approach. Instead, use your storytelling ability to help your readers see in their mind's eye the potential for a new experience, a new way of being, and a new world. They will connect emotionally with the possibility and take it on as their own vision of the future. Memoirs, like Cheryl Strayed's *Wild* or Elizabeth Gilbert's *Eat, Pray, Love*, which inspired many women to go on vision quests of their own, provide examples of such storytelling.

Develop Clarity—People who feel indecisive often lack clarity. The more clarity your readers have about what they want to change, why they want to change it, and their ability to navigate the transformational process, the more likely it is they will decide to act. Think of this like washing the dirty windshield of their cars so they can see the road ahead. Without clarity, they remain immobilized, with their feet firmly on the brake; with clarity, they put their feet on the gas and steer toward their destination.

To help your readers become clear enough to decide, help them understand:

- Their *reasons* (their "why"—the meaning change has for them)
- Their *options* (the tools, strategies, habits, mindsets, or outcomes from which they can choose)
- The *steps* they must take (doing X, Y, and Z to achieve A)

- The *risks* inherent in the process (what they might lose)
- What to *expect* of the process (what the needed action will feel or look like)
- The *outcome* they will achieve (the potential results or benefits of action)

Address each of these items as you write your book. The more clarity you produce in your readers, the more aware they become of the action they must take and the more able they are to decide and take action.

2. Become Influential

Influential people are persuasive. Think of the old advertisement for E.F. Hutton that said, "When E.F. Hutton talks, people listen." That's influence.

The most effective change agents have successfully navigated the process of change and can then demonstrate the possibility of transformation. They serve as role models for the positive aspect of the change they intend to spark and provide living proof that change is attainable.

For instance, Barack and Michelle Obama, the former U.S. President and First Lady, demonstrate what is possible for African Americans. In 2021, Kamala Harris stepped into the U.S. vice president's position and in 2024 ran for president, providing another powerful role model for women of color. Greta Thunberg demonstrates how the conviction of one young person can spur a movement. My friend, who collects the leftover food from gatherings and takes it to the homeless shelter, and my sister, who "adopts" a local family in need each holiday season, both model how individuals can make a difference in others' lives.

If you are in the process of change, you can still be influential. Share the deepest and most challenging parts of your own experience, and readers will relate to and support you—and will feel inspired to join your movement. Even if you are just a few steps ahead on the journey, your audience knows you understand them and their current experience or challenge.

The following three strategies offer ways to increase your influence level.

Change Thoughts and Beliefs—You are in the position to teach your audience how to think differently. That in and of itself makes you an influencer. Your readers will pick up your book to learn something new—not to be told the same things they've heard before. For instance, a CEO who wants to encourage innovation within her company is not looking for tried-and-true strategies.

Thinking differently leads to acting differently. For example, if you want more people to vote in elections but know your readers don't vote because they believe they have no control over who is elected to office, address their most prevalent belief: *My vote doesn't matter.* Provide readers with stories and role models that prove each vote matters and they can make a difference.

Challenge Your Audience—Human beings rise to challenges. For instance, children whose parents have high expectations for them tend to get better grades in school and succeed in life more often than those whose parents hold low expectations for them. So, expect a lot of your readers and challenge them to adopt those expectations for themselves—and rise to meet them.

You have a short time—from your book's first to its last page—to make readers feel supported in stretching beyond their comfort zone. Be the one who cares enough to do that; they will appreciate you for your support.

Challenges can take many forms and should feel doable to the reader rather than overwhelming. Don't ask them to immediately move off the grid, for example; instead, ask them to explore solar panels for their current home or doing research on how to reduce their carbon footprint.

You can challenge a reader with questions, as mentioned previously. For instance: "You may think you cannot change the way your child behaves, but consider that changing your behavior might transform your child's behavior. If that was true, wouldn't it be worth it to you to change your behavior?" And you can challenge them with suggested actions: "Make one small change and see how your child responds."

Search online, and you will find a plethora of three, five, and seven-day challenges offered. They run the gamut from weight loss to intuition development to writing consistently. Each day, participants do one thing to move closer toward a goal. How could you apply this strategy in your book? Perhaps you could end each chapter of your book with a challenge: "Before reading the next chapter, I challenge you to try the strategy I've outlined in this one." Or, like Pam Grout in E^2 and E^3, ask readers to complete an experiment before continuing to read.

Reward and Pressure—Joseph Grenny, coauthor of *Influencer,* claims influence requires a focus on three areas: intrinsic reward, extrinsic reward, and outside pressure. Some people are influenced by extrinsic rewards, meaning things like pay, acknowledgment, and awards. For others, intrinsic reward—a sense of self-worth, progress toward goals, and well-being—proves more powerful. With your reader profile in mind, consider if your readers are more motivated by intrinsic or extrinsic rewards. Then, explain how the change you suggest will provide that. (Knowing where you placed them on the Your Relationship to Change framework will provide insight as well.)

For example, maybe your readers want to lose weight. Write about how doing so will increase their confidence at work and in personal relationships—an intrinsic reward. Also, mention that once they've lost weight, others will notice how great they look—an extrinsic reward.

It's likely your readers already feel outside pressure. In the above example, it is likely that their doctors have told them their weight endangers their health, they find it difficult to play with their children, and their spouses refuse intimacy. When you write about these things in a way that makes your readers relive the discomfort of outside pressure (stirring the pot), their desire for change increases. This is especially true if you tie the benefits of change to the intrinsic or extrinsic rewards your readers will receive when they change.

1. **Reduce Resistance**

Given the likelihood that your readers will have some level of resistance to change, it makes sense to try to lower it. Your readers' resistance may look like refusals to accept or comply with change requests or attempts to prevent change from occurring. They may live comfortable lives and know change might make their situation better but believe it's easier to stay with the status quo. Or they may feel stuck and believe nothing will ever change.

The higher their resistance level, the harder you'll have to work to motivate them to new action. You'll find it easier to author change if you focus your efforts on lowering readers' resistance and increasing their willingness.

Additionally, the following four strategies will help you reduce your audience's resistance to change.

Demonstrate Understanding and Compassion—Before you try to persuade your readers to change, accept them for who and where they are. You don't need to condone their current behavior, but show compassion and support by acknowledging that like you, they are human. Let them know you, too, have resisted change, and share how you moved out of resistance and the benefits of having done so.

Demonstrate understanding. Revisiting an earlier example, you might write, "I understand your frustration with the election system. The system doesn't always seem to work, and it appears impossible to elect an independent—even if he or she is the best candidate. You feel as if you must vote for the lesser of two evils, and sometimes even that vote seems to count for nothing. This is especially true when we see there is outside influence in our election process and that even a three-year-old can hack into the system." Your readers will nod their heads and say, "Yes! That's exactly right...and it's why I don't vote."

Next, present the possibility that something could be different. "Imagine if enough people voted for an independent...and that candidate was just a few votes shy of getting elected," you might write; "and you voted and brought to the polls a few more people who feel as you do but decided to vote on the off chance it would make a difference. What if those few votes didn't just make a differ-ence but *all the difference* in the outcome of the election? Would you then choose to vote?" This language helps your readers see what's possible, and as a result, reduces their resistance another notch or two.

Offer a Plan—Many of your readers will feel inspired to change, or even motivated to action—but they will flounder in their efforts if they don't have a step-by-step plan. Your readers want a how-to manual. Therefore, if you provide a strategy that feels doable, you reduce their resistance to change.

Explain your transformation process in a way that leaves them motivated rather than overwhelmed. For instance, I tell writers who aren't writing but want to develop a daily writing habit to begin with a fifteen-minute block of writing time each day or a goal of producing five hundred words daily. That's manageable.

Identify a few needle-moving behaviors that, if adopted by your readers, will lead to change. "Successful change agents don't spread their efforts across ten priorities. They understand that profound change requires a precise focus. Instead, they focus on three or four 'vital' behaviors," says Grenny.

Develop Courage—Lower your readers' resistance level by increasing their courage level. Courage empowers bold action; encourage readers to stop waiting to feel courageous enough to act and instead, make one small, bold move. Afterward, they will feel more confident and able to take another.

According to Grenny, you can boost readers' courage by getting them to answer two essential questions: "Can I do it?" and "Will it be worth it?" To increase the likelihood that your readers answer those two questions affirmatively, share how you did it and the valuable results you achieved. Your audience members will see themselves in your story and recognize their ability to follow in your footsteps and reap similar rewards.

Drive Up Necessity—Sometimes, the only way to encourage others to change is to highlight the necessity of doing so. For instance, maybe you see a need to stop human trafficking, improve marriages, or level up human consciousness. Your consciousness of this need made you decide to become a writer and start a movement. To help your readers realize they *need* change, show them *why* it's imperative they act. Better yet, if you *ask them* to identify the impact of *inaction*, their necessity level will increase.

If you believe greenhouses gases threaten humanity's ability to thrive on Earth, you probably feel something must be done to fix the causes of this problem. That sense of necessity coupled with urgency —the feeling that something *needs* to be done *now*—drives you to action. Necessity becomes a constant presence pushing you to create change.

People fail to achieve goals because they don't have deadlines or do not believe they need to act sooner rather than later; without a time frame and sense of urgency, they wait. I complete a book more quickly when I feel the urgency of a publisher's due date. My students write more in ninety days than they do all year when they participate in my three-month Write Your Transformational Book Challenge. Help your readers feel the pressure to act immediately— to call their congressman, stop drinking alcohol, meditate daily, fix their marriage, or volunteer at a homeless shelter. Help them feel they must do so *today*—not tomorrow.

4. Change Minds

To change behavior, you must change minds. Unfortunately, the human brain is highly effective at maintaining the status quo and preventing new behaviors from being adopted. Yet your brain cells constantly make new neural connections that allow for change. This process, called neuroplasticity, provides enormous potential for change.

In general, humans choose to act out of habit. The brain deems habits "safe" and anything new "unsafe." Therefore, it wants you to maintain the old way of doing things—even when you are aware that doing so doesn't provide benefit. Knowing this, focus your readers' attention on appeasing the brain while developing new ways of thinking and behaving.

The following two methods effectively change minds.

Use Visualization—Visualization is an enormously helpful tool for encouraging change. The brain doesn't know the difference between what you visualize and what you do. In fact, as you imagine yourself doing something such as lifting weights, it fires off messages to the rest of your body as if you were taking that physical action. Repetitive visualization also creates new neural pathways. Thus, the more often your readers visualize themselves participating in the behavior you recommend—and getting desired results—the more they train their brains to feel safe with the new behavior.

It's common for speakers to lead audiences through visualizations that engage the mind, emotions, and senses because the mental images help people to experience change or a desired result. Do the same in your book. Repeatedly ask your readers to see themselves transformed or experiencing part of the transformation process: "Imagine yourself meditating daily," or "Imagine the peace you will experience from meditating daily." Give them mental pictures that help them see and feel what it would be like to live that change, such as, "See yourself feeling calm and relaxed even when work situations get stressful." That's when new brain connections form and change becomes easier.

Change State—A change in the physical, mental, or emotional state helps people change. You can accomplish this by asking an audience to take a deep breath, think about something pleasant (or unpleasant), smile, or jump up and down, for example. When they change their physical, mental, or emotional state, other inner conditions shift in kind.

As you write your book, include exercises to change your readers' state, such as journaling about happy or sad events or taking an action before reading on, which could be completing a challenge or exercise. Telling a particularly scary or emotional story can also accomplish this goal, as can asking readers to imagine (visualize) something that elicits an emotion.

Try writing with an upbeat voice, then a solemn one. Tell a joke now and then. Construct sentences and paragraphs with varying cadences. Tell stories that make readers laugh and cry. Occasionally, drop into a more emotional place, create a sense of urgency and necessity, or stir the pot; and then switch it up with statistics, steps, or an uplifting story.

Also, consider the energy of the change agents you most admire. Maybe it is Gandhi, Martin Luther King, Jr., Daniele Fiandaca, Marjory Stoneman, Mel Robbins, or David Hogg. Do they role model positive or negative approaches, or high or low energy? Listen to their words. Watch their body language. Study how they carry themselves and speak. And pay attention to the audience's reaction to them: What happens to their state? If the role model you chose has published a book, read it; pay attention to the energy fluctuations in the author's words—and your response to those words—as you read. Learn to bring the most effective energy to your writing by modeling the energy of successful Authors of Change.

5. Inspire Congruence

Most people desire a congruent life, one lived in alignment with their best self, values, goals, and beliefs. Identify where your readers experience incongruities in their identity. For instance, your readers want to be people who walk or use public transportation on a spare the air day, but they drive to work anyway.

Incongruence spurs internal stress and discomfort, while congruence seeds harmony and peace. First, make your readers aware of their incongruities; then provide them with a plan for moving into congruence, being the person they want to be, and taking actions aligned with that identity.

Here are three strategies that will move your readers into congruence.

Increase Personal Power—Instill in your readers a sense of personal power: the ability to take control of themselves and their lives. Too often, people believe they do not possess the agency to change anything. In fact, they have the agency but don't choose to exercise it. Instead, they place blame and make excuses for why they cannot be congruent. But blame and excuses disempower them while responsibility empowers them and provides congruence.

Help your readers take responsibility for their actions (or inactions). Let's say you want to motivate your readers to compost. Their excuses might include, "I don't have enough space in my yard," "I don't have time," or "I have no reason to use the composted material." For each excuse, lead them to conclude that they can compost if they decide to do so. You might explain how they can create a small compost pile in the corner of the yard, describe how it will only take them five minutes per day to take compost to their little heap, and suggest the possibility of sharing the compost with community garden members.

Some of your readers' excuses might be tinged with blame, which means they believe change is out of their control. This makes them victims of circumstances: "My partner doesn't want to compost," or "My landlord won't allow me to have a compost bin." Help them see that it is possible to behave congruently by taking responsibility for their decisions and actions. Ask them to brainstorm choices and solutions, such as handling all composting activities themselves and creating compost without a bin so the landlord doesn't complain.

Encourage Self-Integrity—Your readers are probably good at keeping their promises to others but not to themselves. Each time they disappoint themselves by breaking an inner commitment they have made, your readers lose confidence that they can or ever will do what they promise themselves. Help them find ways to live in integrity with their intentions, and they move into congruence as they start and sustain the change process.

Like most of us, your readers know they *should* do something—and may *want* to do it—but they don't do it even though the action is aligned with their values or who they want to be. They don't take the new action even though they tell themselves they will. A good example of this is found in broken new year resolutions, which create internal dissonance that results in low self-worth.

When your readers become aware of how bad they feel about themselves each time they lack self-integrity, they want to change so they can keep their commitments to themselves. To move them toward self-integrity, you could stir that pot or show them what's possible. Ask them to imagine something like this scene: *You go to a small box on your patio or balcony. When you open the lid, inside you find the most amazing organic fertilizer for your plants. It's compost made from the vegetable scraps you discarded months ago. You scoop some of it up and carefully place it in your rose and vegetable pots. Before going inside, you cut a few gorgeous roses to grace your table and pick some robust lettuce, squash, and tomatoes for dinner—and later enjoy the pleasure of eating your own organic produce.* When you help your readers see how to develop self-integrity, they will then keep their promises to themselves and move into congruence.

Create Goals—Humans constantly grapple with their emotional and rational sides. According to Chip and Dan Heath, authors of *Switch*, most of us think our rational side is driving the car, when in fact, it's our emotional side that has its hands on the wheel and its foot on the gas or brake pedal. The rational side is in the passenger seat. You can author change if you write for both the rational and emotional sides of your readers.

Imagine you are writing a book with the intention of reducing obesity in the United States. While rationally your readers want to return to a healthy weight and help their children to do so, emotionally, both parent and child want their ice cream and cake. They may possibly feel safer being overweight or want to eat for comfort, for instance. Thus, you must get readers' minds and hearts working together even though they want different things. If you don't, this constant internal battle for the driver's seat prevents readers from creating healthier habits and a congruent lifestyle for themselves and their children.

Setting goals gets both the emotional and rational sides on the same page. Still, new habits won't form if your readers don't feel the pressure of a deadline (urgency). A realistic goal, such as losing ten pounds over three months, however, helps the emotional and rational sides work together. The goal provides the emotional side with motivation and the rational side with direction. A specific road both can travel could involve utilizing a health app, a weekly session with a nutritionist, making entries in a calorie journal, or a daily walking regimen.

Now you possess a foundational understanding of how you change, how others change, and how your readers change. You are armed with various strategies to help readers change by increasing their awareness of the need to create change, becoming an influencer in their lives, reducing their resistance to change, changing their minds, and inspiring them to congruence. Use this knowledge to write a book that can change the world and to influence yourself to step more fully into your new identity as an Author of Change.

4

BECOME AN AUTHOR
OF CHANGE

"The more you see yourself as what you'd like to become and act as if what you want is already there, the more you'll activate those dormant forces that will collaborate to transform your dream into your reality."

— WAYNE DYER

Even if you don't consider yourself a writer, haven't published a book, or just got the idea for a book that could make a difference, embody your role as a writer and change agent right now. Show up "as if" you are already an Author of Change. Dress the part, talk the talk, do the things, fake it till you make it. Be an Author of Change—take that on as your identity.

Writing a book that makes a difference requires performing a multitude of roles. Each one helps you fulfill your purpose and your book's purpose. No matter how you publish or the subject of your book, authors today do much more than write.

Thus, becoming an author often requires personal change. For instance, you might need to transform yourself into someone who can fill the following roles:

- **Community Builder**—someone who brings like-minded people together to work for a cause.
- **Reader-Engagement Expert**—someone who knows how to encourage readers and social media followers to write book reviews, leave social media comments, share social media posts, and click on book purchase links.
- **Promoter or Marketer**—someone who can write marketing copy such as emails, sales pages, or ads, and who uses tools that move people towards book purchases.
- **Public Relations Agent**—someone who can be the "face" of a book or movement, create goodwill in a target market or community, write press releases, and contact publications for free media opportunities.
- **Inspirer of Action**—someone with the ability to move people to new action.
- **Professional Speaker**—someone who tells stories and offers information or presentations from the stage in a manner that inspires and motivates an audience to new beliefs, mindsets, and actions.
- **Businessperson**—someone savvy about the workings of the publishing industry and selling books, products, and services; an entrepreneur who can generate income to sustain the message.
- **Content Expert**—a person with the ability to produce valuable written content for books, blog posts, emails, newsletters, videos, infographics, visuals, audio products and video products, speeches, and social media posts.
- **Leader**—a visionary, role model, and teacher who can provide people with a path to get from where they are to where they want to go.

- **Social Media Manager**—someone who understands social media sites and how to use them, including which social media channels best suit a message and who will post on them for you.
- **Influencer**—a person who is known, liked, and trusted within a specific market and therefore has the ability to influence that audience's beliefs and behaviors; a leader with visibility, reach, and authority within a specific market.
- **Expert**—an influential authority or thought leader on a specific topic or in a particular industry.
- **Media Personality**—someone who often appears on radio, television, podcasts, or live Internet events or who hosts a show or station.
- **Author**—a writer who has published a book.
- **Educator**—someone who educates others on a subject in a physical or online classroom.
- **Trainer**—an educator who provides strategies and practical tools or skills meant to accomplish a specific goal.
- **Publisher**—someone who produces and distributes books.

You do not have to take on every one of these roles, but publishing success depends upon adopting at least a few of them, like author, community builder, and promoter. If doing all the tasks required of these roles feels too overwhelming, remember you do not have to do them alone. You can hire help. For example, many people prefer not to spend their time on social media sites like Facebook, Bluesky, or Instagram. If that's you, opt to hire a social media manager. If you feel confident writing a book, email, or blog post but not a press release or copy for a sales page, hire a public relations expert or a copy writer. If you don't know anything about how to publish a book, engage someone who specializes in assisted self-publishing. Many writers begin on a shoestring—including myself—and play every role to the best of their ability. You can do the same until you develop streams of income that sustain your message, or you can invest in support early and put your energy and attention on authoring change.

Keep this in mind: Writers prefer to stay at home and write, while changemakers and activists prefer to be out in the world advocating for change. To write a book that makes a difference, shift gears between both worlds and the activities that go with them. Step into and *embrace* these roles to become an Author of Change.

Who are You Now?

Let's start where you are. Sometimes taking an inventory and realizing that you already are who you need to be provides the confidence to step into new roles. Who are you at this moment? What roles do you fill on a regular basis? Maybe you already write daily—so you are a writer, or you've published a book—and you are therefore an author. Possibly you are an inspirer of action, like a coach, speaker, healer, therapist, or a leader in your industry. Create a chart like the one below in your journal. Then, check off the roles you have filled to date or are currently filling and those you need to step into in the future.

Role	Now	Future
Writer		
Author		
Change Agent		
Community Builder		
Reader–Engagement Expert		
Promoter/Marketer		
Public Relations Agent		
Inspirer of Action		
Professional Speaker		
Bussinessperson		
Content Expert		
Leader		
Social Media Manager		
Influencer		
Expert		
Media Personality		
Educator		
Trainer		
Publisher		

Don't worry if your evaluation comes up with more marks in the future column than in the now column. As you read on, you'll learn how to step into these roles confidently. However, knowing the roles you need to master provides clarity, which means you can make decisions, create a plan of action, and move toward mastery.

For example, if you need to become a social media manager, you might decide to tackle this role first. That decision starts your change process. Next, determine what you need to learn to become excellent at this job. Then, decide to educate yourself—take a course, read a book, or hire a coach. These actions make it possible for you to create a social media strategy, open social media accounts, and begin sharing information and building the audience for your book.

Watch for mindset issues that arise as you begin to fill your new roles. Knowing you must do more than what you are currently doing to transform your readers or their lives and to transform yourself into an author can feel overwhelming. In fact, the first challenge you face might be finding the willingness to be more than you are right now—*to change yourself.* You have to influence *yourself* to take on more duties and do things differently. If you see each new role or necessary action as one that moves you closer to becoming the author of a book that makes a difference, you are more likely to embrace these tasks with enthusiasm.

This is where an Author Attitude helps enormously. I wrote about this mindset in *The Author Training Manual.* It is created by a combination of willingness, optimism, objectivity, and tenacity.

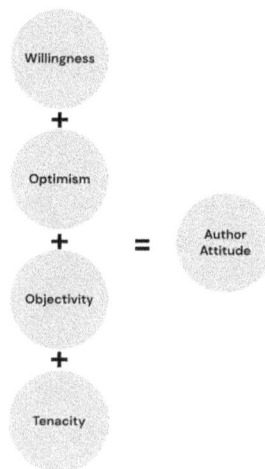

Willingness

+

Optimism

+   =   Author
                Attitude

Objectivity

+

Tenacity

Willingness is the quality or state of being in which you are prepared to do something. You are ready—recall the Stages of Change framework from Chapter 3. This mindset helps you embrace the challenge of doing what is necessary for success. Willingness helps you avoid feeling overwhelmed or stuck and increases your ability to embrace those feelings as part of the process.

Optimism encompasses hopefulness and confidence about the future or a successful outcome. An optimistic mindset has been proven repeatedly to help people succeed. Sometimes optimists seem unrealistic, but that's what drives us forward even when things seem dire. Optimists persevere and don't take failure or rejection personally, and they focus on aspirations and move toward realizing them.

Objectivity means you are not influenced by personal feelings or opinions when considering and representing facts. Writers must be objective when working with editors and publishing professionals and see themselves and their work through the eyes of their readers. You also must see your audience objectively to best address their needs.

Tenacity is enormously important. If you are tenacious, you possess determination and persistence. You don't give up—no matter what setbacks or challenges arise, including rejections from agents or publishers. For example, making the journey from idea to published book can take several years...or longer. The book you hold in your hands is proof of that fact. I had the idea many years before I sold the book to a publisher. Even after I signed a publishing contract, there were ups and downs that required sheer doggedness; but I never gave up on the idea or the project. If I had, this book would not exist. That's tenacity!

Together, all four traits—willingness, optimism, objectivity, and tenacity—create a mindset that leads to successful authorship. Approach your new roles with an author attitude, and you'll have an easier time creating transformation—both in yourself and for your readers.

To determine if you have an author attitude, rate yourself on a scale of one to ten (with ten being the highest) in these qualities and record the results in your journal:

Willingness
1   2   3   4   5   6   7   8   9   10
Optimism
1   2   3   4   5   6   7   8   9   10
Objectivity
1   2   3   4   5   6   7   8   9   10
Tenacity
1   2   3   4   5   6   7   8   9   10

If you score a five or less in any category, don't stress! Ask yourself why you scored so low, and do some journaling about your answer. Keep in mind that low scores provide you with information about where you need improvement and an opportunity to create a plan to level up those scores. Brainstorm strategies to create growth in areas where it is needed, and then act on one or more of them.

To strengthen your author attitude, answer the following set of questions in your journal. Your answers will identify how willing you are to take on some of the roles that will help you succeed. Specifically, record any new insights into what it will take for you to become an author.

- Why do you want to take on new roles?
- If you don't want to take on additional roles beyond writer or author, why don't you want to do so? What stops you?
- How can you increase your desire to adopt new roles?
- How does *not* taking on new roles prevent your success and the success of your book?

- If you don't take on at least a few necessary roles, what does that mean to you? What does it mean to your potential readers?

Many writers allow fear to stop them in their tracks, for instance. In order to make a difference, you must show up authentically in your writing and as a leader, role model, and motivator. That thought alone might fill you with fears around failure, success, being seen, being judged, or being called an impostor. Fear can show up as procrastination, lack of motivation, and/or indecision. Therefore, it's essential to deal with fear—as well as anything else stopping you from becoming an Author of Change.

Any limiting belief, negative outlook, or unsupportive mindset holds you back. If you believe that "It's hard to become a published author," "No one wants to change," or "Change is hard," for instance, you're going to find it difficult to take steps toward your own goals or to convince anyone else to do the same. Additionally, you must overcome negative thoughts like "I don't know enough," "I'm not good enough," or "I'm not a writer." There are many techniques that can help you to change your mindsets and habits, including hypnosis, therapy, and coaching.

Your Definition of Success

Remember, it's not necessary to take on every one of the roles above. However, the more roles you step into—or assign to a team member —the higher the likelihood your attempts to author change will succeed. But success is relative. There is no one-size-fits-all definition of successful authorship, and you get to define success.

However, you already defined success earlier when you created your purpose statement and the purpose statement for your book. You might have additional success markers, such as money earned from your book, lifestyle changes due to becoming an author, or even authority or influence gained by starting a movement. No matter your definition, you must be willing and ready to do what it takes—to become the type of person who can take the necessary actions to achieve that goal.

Your definition of success revolves around your purpose, which dictates the types of roles you'll need to adopt to achieve success. From a publishing industry perspective, a successful book is one that sells enough copies to earn back an advance on sales and the cost of producing the book—and then some. More often than not, books deemed "successful" are bestsellers, which means they sell more than the average number of copies for a new title and outsell their competition. For an Author of Change, a successful book is one that, once read, motivates change and results in change. However, for you, success might mean anything from changing one life to leaving behind a legacy or starting and sustaining a movement.

The publishing industry's definition of success—book sales and revenue—may not be yours. In your journal, define what successful authorship of a change-inspiring book means to you. Describe all aspects of success, including the impact on your life and career, and write about success as *if you've already achieved it*, vividly enumerating what becomes possible if you and your book fulfill your purpose and you achieve your personal authorship goals.

Now, go back and review the list of potential roles you need to take on. Which roles do you want to learn more about and step into? Gauge whether your level of willingness has increased.

Seven Roles *Every* Author of Change Must Play

While you are always at choice about what you do or don't do, seven roles are indispensable. You must be a writer, or at a minimum, work with a ghostwriter to produce a manuscript. Plus, you need to become a businessperson, marketer, expert, influencer, and leader. I have not included change agent in this list of the essential roles because for someone who wants to write a change-inspiring book, that's a given.

Let's look at all seven roles more carefully, starting with the most basic one—that of writer.

1. Writer

Writers write. To be a writer, you must develop a consistent—even daily—writing habit. You can choose to write many types of content to help you advance your cause and your book's success. You can produce emails, blog posts, press releases, and articles, for instance. You can write ebooks and print books, short and long books, but you must write.

If you don't consider yourself a writer, this is the first role to tackle. Set aside time daily to write. Begin work on your manuscript (more on how to structure and develop a content plan for your book in Chapter 10). You also might practice your writing craft in any of the ways mentioned above, such as producing a daily or weekly blog post.

Even if you choose to work solely on your book manuscript, do so unfailingly. Block out daily writing time on your calendar. Many writers find it most conducive to write first thing in the morning before people and tasks demand your attention. Write for an hour or two (or more), if you can. If you find that amount of time difficult to fit into your schedule, set aside time for at least a fifteen to thirty minute session each day, but write consistently.

The more you write, the more you develop the identity of a writer. I had a client who called to say, "I finally get it! I'm a writer."

"What changed?" I asked.

"I write daily."

If you've never considered yourself a writer, now is the time to take on that identity. And if you have always been a writer, step it up! Write more or for new audiences, such as on Facebook, Bluesky, LinkedIn, or even Instagram. Write for publications and blogs.

If you feel uncertain about your writing ability, keep this in mind: You can hire an editor. Many books are written by less-than-talented writers; you'd never know it because the author hired a fabulous editor who cleaned up their manuscript.

Other books aren't even written by the so-called author. Many times, non-writers have a good book idea and hire ghostwriters to produce the manuscript. Some change agents are speakers—not writers; if that describes you, speak your book and then have the transcript of the recording edited into a book by an editor or a ghostwriter.

Don't let your negative self-talk—"I'm not a writer" or "I'm not a good writer"—keep you stuck. You can become an Author of Change, and a successful one at that.

2. Businessperson

Many writers and change agents don't consider themselves busi-nesspeople, yet filling this role leads to the greatest degree of publishing success. Becoming an *authorpreneur*—or even a *changepreneur*— supports your efforts from the moment you decide to publish a book until it gets into the hands of readers and beyond. Plan your book's content with an eye toward marketability by putting together a business plan that includes market research, a competitive analysis, and a marketing plan for the period before and after publication. Additionally, you can create a strategy to monetize your book with courses, coaching, speaking, and membership sites.

An entrepreneurial approach allows you to create income to sustain your movement and reach more people with your message.

Before publishing your book, it's crucial to determine how you will bring your book to market. To make that decision, you must know if you would make a good publishing partner or a savvy publisher. Traditional publishers want to work with good writers who have great ideas and have created an engaged community of potential readers or an author platform. These are people in your target market ready and waiting to purchase the book upon its release. (For ways to build an author platform, read Chapters 6, 7, and 8.)

If you choose to take the self-publishing route, it's imperative that you become business minded. After all, you'll be stepping into the role of "publisher" and running a publishing company that produces, distributes, and markets your books. You must know how to manufacture high-quality books like those brought to market by traditional publishers, which means gathering and working with a team of professionals, including editors and designers. Plus, you must have an author platform and understand book marketing. (Learn more about both traditional publishing and self-publishing in this book's conclusion.)

3. Marketer

Marketing falls into the realm of business. However, it's a specific function all writers must perform (or hire someone to perform for them). No matter how you publish, you need to understand the different ways to market your book to your target audience, and you must be willing and able to take these strategic actions or hire an expert to assist in these tasks.

Marketing involves a wide range of activities that continuously give your audience value. Done well, the result is simple: Your audience purchases your book and joins your movement. Each book you publish needs a separate marketing plan.

Marketing activities include market research, competitive analysis, book and product positioning, pricing, and any efforts to keep your book in the minds of potential readers and stimulate demand. Used as an umbrella term, marketing includes advertising, which is a "paid" effort (such as running a Facebook ad), and publicity, which is a "free" effort, including activities like getting media mentions or making a radio appearance.

Your marketing plan includes your strategy for reaching potential readers and selling your book over time, not just during a launch. This could mean building a mailing list, running ads on a free video series, or social media posts and ads.

Many writers, coaches, healers, and change agents believe a focus on marketing cheapens their work and goes against their values. In fact, melding this role with writing and a desire to be of service allows you to author change more effectively. Always remember that marketing helps you sell books, which allows you to reach and impact your audience. It enables you to fulfill your purpose and that of your book.

A business approach allows you to see the big picture of your book project. When you have your purpose and the book's purpose at the forefront of your mind, you are more likely to create a salable book related to a viable cause—and do what is necessary to get it in front of your audience. Ultimately, the role of marketer enables you to determine both your immediate and future needle-moving steps toward achieving your mission and purpose.

4. Expert

Many writers don't feel like experts, but everyone knows something about something—usually a lot more than someone else. That makes you an expert. There is no need for impostor syndrome—the internal belief that you are faking your own authority—to hold you back, especially not when you know enough about a topic to write a book. You have something important to share, and your message can make a difference.

Plus, expert status is not only about credentials. You don't have to have a diploma, certification, or even a lot of experience to be seen as an expert. You do, however, need a strong, unique, and powerful strategy for change. Then, it's your job to share that strategy and demonstrate how it leads to transformation. Do that often, and people see you as an expert.

I was not considered a blogging expert until I started a blog about blogging books. The more often I wrote and published on this topic, the greater my status became as an authority on blogging, blogging books, landing traditional book publishing deals, and book marketing. The same is true of my status as a nonfiction writing expert. I was given that title after blogging on the topic on my *Write Nonfiction Now!* blog site for many years and running the Write Nonfiction in November (WNFIN) Challenge, also known as National Nonfiction Writing Month (NaNonFiWriMo). My expert status provided opportunities to speak at writing and blogging conferences, write for major websites and magazines, and earn a living as a nonfiction editor and a blogging and writing coach. It also helped me to land my first traditional publishing book deal, as well as others that followed, and to sell copies of those books. A book written by an expert is more likely to be purchased by someone seeking an authority to teach them how to do something.

Additionally, expert status helps you gain influence with your audience because you have the "know-like-trust" factor: If you market yourself well, you provide potential readers the chance to *know* you. If they *like* you and the information you share, they are more likely to *trust* you. And if they trust you, they will buy your book and take up your cause.

Write Your Author of Change Bio

Your author bio appears inside or on the back cover of your book, on your website, at the end of your guest blog posts and magazine articles, and in promotional materials for your book, talks, and appearances, as well as in all literature about your movement.

Compose your Author of Change bio either in your journal or a computer document. Include not only important items from your resume or professional experience but also accomplishments or areas of focus that demonstrate your expertise and that explain why you have taken on your mission or cause. Concentrate on the aspects of your life and experience that make you an authority on the type of change you want to inspire.

Look at the bios of other people who have written about a cause they believe in. Find the description of their mission on their websites or in their published books. Use these as examples of how to write your bio and opportunities to determine how you differ from other authors.

Here's another way to get started. In your journal, create a chart like the example below. List three of your most significant accomplishments along with the reason why this makes you the best person to write your book. Then, use the details to begin writing your bio. What have you done in your life or career that is notable and that makes you an expert in the subject area of your book?

Accomplishment	Reason this makes you an expert

Write your bio in the third person. Include your credentials and life experience as they pertain to your book's subject matter. Add less pertinent information toward the end.

When finished, you should feel a sense of accomplishment, expertise, and authority. Additionally, you will realize you are not an "impostor," but rather a true expert with an important message to share.

5. Influencer

You motivate people to change when they see you as a trusted authority. Who are the influencers in your life? Do you listen to what they say and act on their recommendations? I bet you do because you see them as wise or distinguished in their field.

Strive to be *the* influencer in your readers lives; then they'll take up your brand of change and become part of your movement. Imagine your audience reading your book and then taking action, thereby becoming your army of change agents. For that to happen, they must pay attention when you tell them your book is available for purchase and buy it—because you are influential in their lives. These readers also need to act on the recommendations in your book.

Consider once more the influencers in your life, such as your parents. Perhaps you still hear your mother or father's voice in your head. It could be that your spouse, your sister, or a friend influences how you think or behave. Maybe it's a teacher, coach, or politician that impacts what you do or don't do.

I recall Jake Hubbard, my college magazine journalism professor, telling me to "figure it out." I couldn't get an editor at a major magazine to talk to me for a class project. He explained, "In the real world, your editor would expect you to find a solution. So, find one." To this day, I figure things out! If there's a problem, I look for a solution. My mother also had a solution orientation. These two influencers in my life helped me become a problem solver.

Obviously, you can influence others in positive or negative ways. Work to focus on positive change. One of my longtime clients once told me, "When I'm seeking an answer related to my book project, my husband asks me, 'What would Nina say?'" You want your readers to think of you as the kind of person who influences others positively and has the answers. When they do, you will impact their lives in powerful ways;

in fact, they'll not only take on your change strategies but will also share them with others. As a result, additional people will be introduced to you and your work, which means your reach and authority will grow.

6. Leader

Your level of influence directly impacts your ability to lead your movement. Whatever your cause, you need to be its biggest advocate and march at the front of the pack to guide those who follow.

Every movement has a leader at the helm. Change agents typically understand this and step up to guide the ship even if somewhat reluctant. However, many writers don't see themselves as leaders, which causes them to avoid risks and limit themselves. For your book to have the impact you desire, step into a leadership role. Enlist those who desire change, and once they have signed on, lead them. And even if you don't yet have anyone to lead...so far, lead anyway. Be a leader.

Writers are leaders. Words have impact. Books make a difference. Own your leadership role and use it to do good in the world.

7. Change Agent

A change agent is someone who promotes, champions, supports, and enables change to happen within a group or organization. Change agents are responsible citizens who win the respect and acceptance of other citizens, and as a result, create successful movements. Sometimes they are activists who protest social conditions and institutional practices that violate core societal values and principles. They also educate, organize, and involve the public to actively change present policies and seek positive, constructive solutions. Finally, agents of change can be reformers who work with political and judicial structures to incorporate solutions into new laws and the practices of public and private institutions.

Beyond these commonly held definitions, change agents are those who actively try to create positive change on any level. They might work to bring about personal, organizational, or community transformation in areas that have little to do with global or governmental issues. They inspire and motivate people from all walks of life to think and behave in new ways.

Obviously, if you plan to write a book that makes a difference—that inspires and motivates people to change—you must be a change agent. You don't have to be an activist or reformer, although you might want to take on these identities.

Don't Sell Your Soul to Succeed as an Author

For eight years, I built my author platform by blogging and sharing on social media sites. However, I did so because I was "supposed to;" it was necessary to land a traditional publishing deal. When the traditional publishing deal didn't come, I was ready to give up. But readers told me that my posts made a difference in their lives, which was the goal I wanted to accomplish with my books. So, I started to look at my role as a blogger and social media thought leader as a way to get my message out sooner—rather than later—and to help achieve my authorship goals. This shift in mindset had a profound effect on my success. In fact, four years later, I held my first tradition-ally published book in my hands—a book that inspired many people.

Embrace the additional roles necessary for successful authorship. (You might even find you enjoy some of them!) You may feel that focusing on sales, marketability, leadership, and community building makes you less spiritual or virtuous than you'd like, but it doesn't cheapen your art or intentions. Instead, it makes you someone who knows that stepping out in these ways helps you to reach more people, make a greater impact, and ensure your move-ment lasts long after the book is published. That's how willingly taking on these roles helps you to fulfill your purpose and that of your book.

Filling these roles doesn't make you less of a writer either. Stepping into them makes you a savvy writer who understands the makings of a successful book. It makes you a writer who knows how to get books into people's hands and cares enough about making a differ-ence in the world to do what's necessary to produce a marketable book—a book that sells, gets read, and makes an impact.

You can live into each role fully while you are still a writer and change agent and remain grounded in your values and purpose. In fact, melding these tasks into your work as a writer allows you to express things that matter most to you. Your purpose will guide your project and actions—even the identities you take on. The more you stay true to yourself, trust that you are doing the best for your cause and book, and align with your purpose, the more each action you take brings you closer to expressing your authentic and best self.

You don't need to sell your soul to succeed as an author. Instead, allow the process of becoming an author to feed your soul and help you fulfill your purpose.

Align Your Values with Authorship

If you continue to feel as if taking on any or all of the roles mentioned in this chapter is misaligned with your values, clarify those values. In your journal, make a list of your top ten values in order of importance. For example, your list might include service, family, honesty, spiritual connection, or hard work.

Once you have a list of your values, describe why each one is important to you. For instance, you might write: *Service is important to me because I feel everyone has something to offer, and it's important to share your gifts with those in need.*

Next, answer this question: *How can I align the roles I must take on to author change with my purpose and values?* Your answer to this question will guide you toward the congruent action you are willing and inspired to take.

Every role you step into provides an opportunity to focus on how the tasks it involves help you fulfill your purpose and live into your values. What does this role mean to you and the success of your book project—or your entire movement? Stay focused on the goal and on being of service. Remember why you started this journey: You want to author the change you want to see in the world.

To do that, you need a new identity. You need to be an Author of Change.

NINA AMIR

Evaluate Your Feelings About Becoming an Author of Change

Take some time to evaluate how you now feel about becoming an
Author of Change. In your journal, answer the following questions
and record any insights, feelings, or concerns:

- *Do you feel you need to change your level of willingness
  concerning any specific areas or roles related to becoming an
  author or an Author of Change?*
- *Are you ready and willing to move forward now and author
  change?*
- *Can you fully step into the identity of Author of Change?* (This
  means adopting some of the roles described in this
  chapter.)

Sometimes you must look at what you have at stake before you
commit to your dreams. Journal your answers to the following questions to increase your level of commitment to authoring change:

1. What might I lose if I *don't* become the type of person who
   can author change?
2. What might I gain if I *do* become the type of person who can
   author change?

Fear represents one of the major deterrents to achieving goals. Take
some time to write endings to the following sentence-completion
exercises and uncover the fears that hold you back:

3. What I fear about success is...
4. What I fear about failure is...
5. What I fear about showing up and letting people see me is...
6. What I fear about leading a cause or movement is...
7. What I fear about becoming an Author of Change is...
8. What I fear about taking on the role of _____ is...

Track Your Tasks Back to Purpose

Allow your purpose to guide you and you will maintain your creativity, passion, inspiration, and spiritual connection for your book project. You will find many tasks and roles fall into place under the umbrella of your purpose. As a result, you will be willing to take on non-writing related tasks and will find them more enjoyable and relevant to your endeavor.

Most of the necessary tasks and roles also fall under the identity of Author of Change. As you tackle them, every day you will feel more and more like someone who writes books that make a difference.

When you find yourself feeling put off by certain tasks that you don't perceive as personally meaningful to you or aligned with your purpose or values, find a path back to your goal by asking yourself powerful questions. For instance, answer these:

- How does doing that job help me fulfill my purpose? And how does it help my book fulfill its purpose?
- How will accomplishing that task help me to author change or to become an Author of Change?
- What brings me back to my center point of serenity and groundedness?
- What can I do that might help me feel willing to take on these tasks? (Answers might include such steps as meditation, reminding yourself of how that action helps you to achieve your goal, or speaking with a potential reader.)

In your journal, list the tasks or jobs that feel empty or misaligned for you, and then track how they can help you fulfill your purpose. For instance, maybe you dislike the idea of using Threads on Instagram. You've refused to get on this social network for years because you don't want the distraction or the lack of privacy you believe comes with use of a social network. Now, flip your thinking. Consider how Threads provides a useful tool for reaching your target audience. Imagine creating a Threads group and inspiring change for the people who join it. See your use of Threads as a business decision aligned with your purpose, one that helps you connect with ideal readers. Would using this social network then feel more appealing?

Pay attention to what tasks or jobs don't feel in alignment with your higher purpose. Try to discern whether they are not right for you or if it is only fear telling you not to do them. Explore this in your journal.

It is possible to approach all the roles necessary for becoming an Author of Change in an aligned manner that fulfills your purpose. Each needed task or action can serve your audience and help you to be of service. If a task draws more people to your cause or assists you in getting a step closer to finishing your manuscript or getting your book published, consider that it is a necessary priority that is aligned with your core values. For example, focus on how activities like marketing, creating a business plan, or building an author platform connect to your mission.

Here's the bottom line: Your success as an author and change agent depends on more than just your writing. If you take on the necessary roles in a manner that feels purposeful and meaningful to you, you'll be able to embrace them. Keep the bigger picture in mind—authoring change—and you will do what it takes with enthusiasm and commitment. Take on the identity of Author of Change. Step into that identity fully, and your mindsets and habits will align with it as well, allowing you to make a positive and meaningful difference with your words.

5

BE THE MESSENGER
AND THE MESSAGE

The most important thing is to try and inspire people so that they can be
great in whatever they want to do.

— KOBE BRYANT

As the adage goes, talk is cheap. Instead of speaking about change, allow people to see you behaving differently and getting desired results. That's how you inspire and motivate through by providing a role model. When you model the change you wish to see in the world, you become a believable example of transformation. As a result, people are naturally attracted to you and your mission.

Gandhi said it best: "If we could change ourselves, the tendencies in the world would also change. As a man changes his own nature, so does the attitude of the world change towards him." This quote is more commonly seen on bumper stickers as, "Be the change you want to see in the world." Indeed, it's not enough to have a message —to author change, you must demonstrate the message.

Every talented inspirational or motivational speaker knows this to be true. I watched the late Sean Stephenson on the stage several times. This American therapist, self-help author, and motivational speaker was born with osteogenesis imperfecta; he stood three feet tall, had fragile bones, and used a wheelchair. Yet he spoke convincingly about becoming happy. He often said, "If I can be happy, so can you."

Consider Jack Canfield; as the author of *Chicken Soup for the Soul*, he has touched millions of people with his advice on how to approach life. I once heard him speak at a writer's conference, and his tenacity inspired me and the rest of the audience to believe we could become authors.

Then there's Tony Robbins, who went from being broke and overweight to becoming a successful speaker, trainer, coach, and author. His story illustrates the ability we each possess to change by learning to control our minds and actions. Robbins teaches that our destiny is determined by our decisions.

Or look up Josh Shipp, an award-winning speaker at events for parents, teachers, caring adults, and young people. Josh was abandoned at birth and placed into many different foster homes. Abused, addicted, and suicidal, he was a teen in trouble. But thanks to his last foster parents, Josh was able to triumph over his hardships. He now teaches that every child is one caring adult away from success. He has dedicated his life to helping adults understand kids and helping kids understand themselves.

You, too, have a story—or more than one—that demonstrates your ability to transform. When you share it, whether aloud or in written form, people will believe they can achieve similar results and will feel inspired and motivated to change. Step into your message and embody it. To do that, you must:

- Take on the change you want to inspire.
- Demonstrate how that change makes a positive and meaningful difference in your life.
- Role model your message with words and actions.
- Create a brand that represents you and your movement.

Everything about you must say, "I am my purpose. I am my mission in action." That's when people see, hear, and understand your message simply by exposure to you. They instantly relate to you within seconds if they land on your website's home page, check out your Bluesky or Instagram feed, or see the cover of your book. They perceive the value you offer each time they see your logo or head-shot. Then, you become a magnet attracting followers, readers, and community members.

Take on Change

You know the type of change you want to promote. However, you might consider yourself an imperfect example of transformation. Maybe you feel uncomfortable telling others to do things differently because you are still in the process of change. Perhaps you get sucked into impostor syndrome and end up feeling like a fake because you haven't perfected the lessons you want to teach.

Teaching what you most need to learn provides a powerful way to change while demonstrating that process. Simply walk your talk: Continue living in the process of change and allow those you'd like to motivate to see you changing. They'll accept your failures and foibles —and your successes—as human, and in response, they will feel more able to transform. After all, if you can keep moving toward transformation, so can they!

I used to be a member of an intermittent fasting group on Facebook. The two women who ran the group sometimes mentioned eating outside their window or eating too much. They then mentioned how they got back to their eating routine. This made each of them a part of the group—another person working toward weight loss and a healthy lifestyle, not someone who had perfected the process.

Sometimes, the most powerful stories are those of someone still in the process of transformation. In *The Dark Side of the Light Chasers,* Debbie Ford reveals how she treated a woman in one of her classes with prejudice. Sharing the story revealed Ford's flaws to the reader and demonstrated how many of us have hidden prejudices we need to acknowledge and heal.

It's okay to be human. (We all are.) Other humans appreciate when role models admit they are like us—flawed. A role model's tenacity around correcting their imperfections inspires us to keep working toward change.

Demonstrate the Positive Effects of Change

Your most important step toward authoring change comes from creating transformation in your own life. Take on the change you want to inspire. Make it part of your daily life. Demonstrate it in public. Become a walking billboard showing others how your desired change makes a difference in your life, the lives of others, or the world.

For example, if you are a woman who wants to empower young girls to become leaders, lead. Don't just speak about empowered leadership in appearances at their schools; be an empowered leader in the community. Show up looking and behaving in a manner that demonstrates your personal power and ability to guide others. Stand tall. Look people in the eye. Be present. Ask empowering questions.

If you want to increase literacy in your country, read...a *lot*...and demonstrate the power of reading, perhaps in YouTube videos, social media posts, libraries, or schools. Share what you learn from each book, start a virtual book club, or create a free video-based program online that teaches people to read. No matter where you go, carry a book. Team up with a group like ProjectLiteracy.com. And of course, tell your story about why you believe reading is so important.

To help you find new ways to demonstrate the change you want to inspire, journal your answers to these questions:

- How can you carry yourself, speak, and gesture as if you *already* lead a community or movement?
- How can you illustrate your cause by how you live your life?
- How can you do a better job of bringing your message or mission to life and embody what you're trying to say?

Role Model Your Message

The previous exercise helps you brainstorm ways to step into your message and embody it. Besides embodiment, your verbal and written messages should also demonstrate your message.

For example, if your type of change is environmental in nature, you could share Facebook, Instagram Live, or YouTube videos showing yourself composting, reducing your carbon footprint, plugging in your electric car, or fertilizing your garden with natural products. You could write an article or blog post about replacing aerosol products with pump sprays. Or you could explain how the clothes you wear are "sustainable fashion" and tell your story of moving to a sustainable community.

If you want to inspire men to take more responsibility for themselves, you could produce videos for YouTube showing how responsibility leads to personal empowerment. You might create a workshop in which you teach related concepts and tell stories from your own experience of making a shift from victim to victor. Share about the difference it made when you became responsible for all aspects of yourself and your life; do this either live with an audience or virtually, and include how doing so changed your self-perception, circumstances, relationships, and results.

Such actions require a huge amount of passion for and commitment to your mission. Everything you do must revolve around two questions:

1. Is this action, behavior, relationship, project, or way of showing up on message for me?
2. Does this action, behavior, relationship, project, or way of showing up demonstrate my purpose or mission?

If you can answer "yes" to those questions, you become a glowing example of change and a beacon to others interested in your mission.

At some point, you want to demonstrate transformation. Transformation is intoxicating. When it comes to marketing, selling transformation offers the highest value. You can demonstrate completed change in others—especially in your clients, customers, or patients, but using your own life as an example is enormously powerful. When people look at you and your life, behavior, and success and feel inspired or motivated to change, you become both the message and the messenger. Focus your efforts on demonstrating how you have successfully navigated the process of change and how that transformation is possible for others. Become the representation of the change you want to inspire.

In your journal, explore how you can inspire and motivate others to follow in your footsteps, take up your cause, or change in some way. Without trying to convince anyone that change is good for them, their organization, their community, or the world, what can you do to encourage them to think or behave differently? Make a list of ways you can become a powerful role model.

For example, if you want people to clean up the oceans and beaches, you could:

1. *Take a walk on the beach every weekend and pick up trash.*
2. *Use social media to share the activities you engage in that help save fish and wildlife affected by trash in the ocean.*
3. *Share photos of yourself involved in volunteer activities for organizations involved in cleaning up the oceans.*

In your journal, make a list of the ways in which you will become a role model. Put a check mark next to three items you commit to pursuing this month.

Next, journal about how you can encourage your audience to think in a new way or to see the world differently. Make a list of the five most essential beliefs your audience must adopt to successfully take on your change and get results. If you need a prompt to help you discover these beliefs, first identify their current belief, and then identify the opposite belief. For instance, *My vote doesn't make a difference* could be transformed to *My vote matters*; or *I am a victim of circumstance* could be shifted to *I am responsible for my life*. For each new, positive belief, come up with one idea for how you can demonstrate the power of that perspective.

For example, if your mission involves helping people navigate the health care system in your country, your list might include the following belief your audience needs to adopt:

1. New belief—*I have the ability to figure out how to navigate the health care system in my country.* (Current belief—*The health care system in my country is confusing, and I don't know how to navigate it.*)

Idea: *Offer social media and blog posts that feature tips for navigating the health care system. Share stories about how you and your clients have learned to navigate the system and how their mindset helped them do so.*

Your turn. Make your list in your journal.

1. Belief—

Idea:

2. Belief—

Idea:

3. Belief—

Idea:

4. Belief—

Idea:

5. Belief—

Idea:

Finally, make a list of five ways to challenge your audience to change. A challenge increases your audience's aspiration for something better. Your challenge should not be confrontational. Instead, show people the difference between where they are and where they want to be and assure them you can help them bridge that gap. Encourage them to create a vision for the future that they feel they must move toward. Create necessity and desire as well as a sense that what they want is achievable.

If your mission is to get more people to adopt intermittent fasting in order to become healthier, you might:

- *Create an online challenge to try intermittent fasting for a month. Invite people to an online kick-off event where you explain how intermittent fasting works and its benefits. Offer this in a Facebook group and encourage participants to share their progress and struggles via comments for thirty days. Each day, offer participants encouragement and motivational posts in the group.*

- *Create an intermittent fasting group in your community. Challenge those who join to choose an accountability buddy and to show up every other week for a check-in. Encourage others to do the same in their own communities. Blog about your experiences and the results achieved by other groups.*

Make your list of five possible challenges in your journal. Detail how you might carry them out.

Create a Distinctive Brand for Yourself and Your Book

Many authors think branding is only for big-box businesses like Target, Barnes & Noble, or Lowe's. You may recognize *brands* like Nike, Amazon, or Apple by their logos and tag lines but may still believe you don't need anything that makes you, your work, and your message recognizable in that manner. In fact, every business needs a brand—and publishing is a business. So is transformation.

You are in the business of transformation as well as the business of publishing. See yourself as a publisher and businessperson as well as a change agent—actively take on those roles. No matter how you publish your book, when it is released, you enter the business of selling books. If you self-publish, you are in essence opening a publishing company, which means you produce, distribute, and sell books—the same thing a traditional publisher does. If you choose to market your book and cause as a speaker, coach, or trainer, you sell services. And should you decide to create online courses or membership sites to further your cause and the education of your audience, you are an authorpreneur. All these scenarios require branding.

Branding is the practice of creating a name, symbol, or design that identifies and differentiates a product from other products. Think of the Nike swoosh, Evernote's elephant, or Apple's apple logo. Imagine how a brand might help your book and anything related to it, such as products and services —as well as your movement—to be understood and noticed. Branding helps the consumer know what a company stands for and understand the value it brings to the market.

To decide how you would like to create a brand for yourself, answer this one question in your journal: How do I want to be known by readers and the public? Asked another way, how do I want my work and movement to be recognized?

Think of the brands you know—Levi's, Ferrari, Honda, Costco, Macy's, Target, or Whole Foods, for example. Each has a recognizable logo and tag line that shouts what marketers call a "unique selling proposition" (USP). For example, Levi's are classic, long-lasting, and comfortable—hence the tagline, "Live in Levi's." Ferraris are fast; and the company website says, "Start your engine." Whole Foods is natural and healthy and focuses on "Whole Foods, Whole People, Whole Planet." Target's brand promise is "Expect More. Pay Less." Honda's car slogan is "We make it simple." It's easy to recognize a company's values, benefits, and characteristics from their branding. While the tagline helps initially, at some point seeing the logo provides a reminder of what the brand represents.

Authors and change agents also have brands and USPs. A website provides an expression of your brand—one that extends to your social media pages as well. Author Jonathan Fields is a great example. Check out his website at https://goodlifeproject.com and discover his "live a better life" movement. On his site you can get involved in that community by purchasing his books, listening to his podcast, reading his blog, or taking his Good Life Bucket Quiz. Or look up author Chris Guillebeau at https://chrisguillebeau.com. His brand tagline is "The Art of Non-Conformity." His movement revolves around "unconventional people doing remarkable things."

Then there's author Gretchen Rubin. Visit her site at https://gretchen rubin.com to find an assortment of books, blogs, and podcast episodes revolving around "happiness and good habits." And if you want an example of a simple brand, look up Greg McKeown at https://gregmckeown.com. His brand message—essentialism, or "the pursuit of less"—is further expressed in his logo and website design, which reflect his book cover design. The simple use of his name and the colors of his book as a logo say, "less is more."

You don't need a logo or tagline, even though they prove helpful. You can create a brand with your body of work, such as a series of books. When enough people know what you stand for, they associate your name with that value. If, for example, you write, speak, and create events around stepping into personal power, eventually, your name becomes associated with personal power.

By creating a brand, you tell the world who you are and how you want to be known. A brand gives you a greater ability to influence how your readers and followers perceive you and your work. In fact, you decide this *for them* in the process of branding. Don't leave that perception to chance. Help your audience come to the decision you desire. If your brand is clear and strong—and your work lines up with that brand—everyone will see you in the way you have chosen.

For instance, don't put your change efforts related to overcoming trauma into the world and merely hope that people will see what you are doing as easily implemented, logical, and backed by science. Instead, create a brand that clearly tells them those are the values, benefits, and characteristics of your movement. Do this with a tagline, a logo, a website, your blog posts and articles, or even some nifty swag, like T-shirts and baseball caps that say, "You are not your trauma." And write a book that offers the same message clearly on its cover.

How Do You Want to Be Known?

Take a big-picture view of the change you want to author. That transformation may start with or extend to your book, but consider the greater effects of your work. How will lives and organizations or even the world be altered as a result of the change you propose? Then, develop a strategy—a brand strategy—that brings your change to life with everything you do, say, or write.

As you go through this chapter's exercises, the best way to become the message and the messenger will become clear to you. Journal about the following questions as you begin thinking about role modeling, branding, and the face you and your book present to the world.

1. How do you want to be known as an author?
2. How do you want your work to be recognized in the world? Is it recognizable now?
3. If your brand had a face—an image—what would it look like? (Think logos, colors, website, pictures, content, and so on.)
4. How would someone describe you?
5. How would someone describe your book?
6. How would someone describe your mission, cause, or movement?
7. Do you currently embody the change you want to see in the world? How?
8. Are you a good role model for the change you want to inspire? Why?
9. What makes you special or unique?
10. What makes your movement different?

Now, look over your answers and consider how you might intentionally use some of this information to create a memorable public perception of you, your book, and your mission or purpose. Remember: you want your author brand to leave a lasting impression so that you, your book, and your movement are easily recognized.

Think beyond logos, websites, social media presence, and brand statements. Consider creating a brand for you and your book that is fully expressed visually, verbally, graphically, and in writing. For instance, your personal style provides an expression of your brand. Your clothing, hairstyle, behavior, speech, gestures, and posture all reflect your values, professionalism, leadership style, and personality —and your brand. Your appearance and style choices leave an impression and send a message to your audience.

Be bold about showcasing your unique style and personality—especially if doing so supports your branding. If you need a makeover, give thought to whether you should consult your hair stylist or barber, seek help choosing a new wardrobe and visiting a clothing store, or hire a personal brand coach. Additionally, consider hiring a vocal coach. Sometimes a change in how you speak allows your message to be heard more effectively.

Take an objective big-picture look at yourself and your work. If you struggle with your branding, seek professional help or ask people you trust for assistance. Explain your movement and the message you want to convey. Request feedback on whether your current appearance and ways of speaking and behaving fit your cause and your leadership role in that movement.

It's easy to look at people you see on the television news or on media award programs and assume personal branding came easily to them. But they each became representatives of their brand after much thought and attention. They created public perception intentionally. You need only look at a show like *America's Got Talent* (or check out the similar shows in many other countries). Watch as the participants change their style—even slightly. They are coached in how to be seen in a way that helps them succeed. As an author and leader of a movement—even if that movement's mission is to get people walking every day, praying more frequently, composting regularly, or voting in elections—it becomes even more important to see yourself as a leader and to act and dress the part.

Don't fall into the trap of thinking you aren't a leader and that therefore, you don't need to worry about how you look. You are leading a movement—whether it revolves around creating profitable churches, better marriages, conscious kids, better food labeling, more stringent gun laws, financially savvy divorced women, or reductions in greenhouse gases. No matter what, be yourself. Your audience will know immediately if you are inauthentic.

Don't worry about getting your branding right the first time around. It's great if you can do it effectively right off the bat, but a brand can be changed. I've seen numerous successful businesspeople and celebrities change their branding...more than once. Think of Prince, who in 1993, changed his stage name to an unpronounceable "Love Symbol." Or consider Madonna, who changed her look almost every year to match a song, or Taylor Swift, who tore apart her earlier brand as the loveable girl next door to grow up, along with her audience, into a sometimes angry and often more risqué adult. Not everyone manages to get their branding right the first time. If your audience likes and trusts you, they will grow with you and your brand.

Two Essential Branding Tools

Once you have an idea of the brand image you want to convey, it's time to turn to two essential branding tools: written and verbal messages. Let's explore each one.

All your written content needs to be "on brand." However, when looking at your book or your content marketing strategy, which includes blog posts, videos, social media updates, ebooks, infographics, newsletters, case studies, or interviews, tie everything together. The most powerful content marketing revolves around a strategic approach that focuses on the creation and distribution of valuable, relevant, and consistent content meant to attract and retain a clearly defined audience. You also want that content to inspire action—to produce readers and members of your movement.

Every bit of content you produce equates to a chance to market your book and cause; but that does not mean directly selling to your audience. Your emails, posts, articles, and YouTube videos must provide benefit. Additionally, pack your content with solid arguments and data that validate your cause.

When creating your content marketing strategy, build in stories that help your audience see your transformation or your commitment to your cause. These provide glimpses into how change has manifested results in your life, your client's lives, organizations, communities, or elsewhere in the world, and how it has turned your struggles into lessons, solutions, and answers. As such, these stories become powerful brand messages.

A good example of this type of brand message is Brendon Burchard's car accident. He shares how he stood bleeding on the hood of the car and asked himself three questions: Did I live? Did I love? Did I matter? As a result of the accident, he focused his life on helping people live lives of meaning and service, and out of that experience came his brand motto: "Live. Love. Matter."

That brings us to verbal messages. Storytelling is a powerful way to convey a message. An April 2018 *Forbes* article quoted Eric Danetz, Global Chief Revenue Officer at AccuWeather, saying: "High-quality, authentic storytelling is critical in today's fragmented media environment. With noise and competition for consumer attention and brands targeting for greater personalization and impact, storytelling becomes key to establishing an emotional connection with your audience. In terms people and businesses can relate to, storytelling illustrates how a brand will meet customers' needs, and in turn, builds loyalty."

For storytelling to work as a brand strategy, however, it must come off as authentic. Despite your focus on intentionally creating public perception, you still must be perceived as real. More than that, you must *be* real as you employ basic storytelling tactics from the world of writing.

Tell Great Stories

Storytelling is not just about entertaining your readers. A well-told story helps your audience understand and identify with complicated concepts and create strong connections faster than other approaches. It gives your readers clarity, which supports their making decisions and taking action.

Good storytellers quickly create strong connections with their audiences. There's science to back up the need to tell stories to connect with and motivate your audience. Psychologist Uri Hasson of Princeton University researches the neurological basis of human communication and storytelling. He discovered some interesting facts about how our brains respond to stories. Functional magnetic resonance imaging (fMRI) from his lab reveals that our brains show similar activity when more than one of us hear the same story. In one study, five people listened to the same personal story told aloud. Before the recording began, their brains showed varied activity. Once the story started, however, their brain activity synced up, or became what Hasson calls "aligned."

Since stories align us with others and help us understand concepts, there are good reasons to make storytelling part of how you share your message. The best sales methods involve storytelling. Consider Super Bowl television commercials as an example. Keith Quesenberry, a lecturer at Johns Hopkins Center for Leadership Education, studied the effectiveness of over one hundred Super Bowl commercials and successfully predicted that the commercials that told the clearest stories would be the most likely to go viral. Indeed, a Budweiser commercial featuring a puppy who made friends with a Clydesdale got more traction than any other ads. This spot condensed an entire story into thirty seconds—puppy and horse meet and become friends, puppy is adopted, horse rallies other horses to stop people from taking puppy away, and puppy remains on the farm with horse. In the article, Quesenberry explains, "People think it's all about sex or humor or animals, but what we've found is that the underbelly of a great commercial is whether it tells a story or not...The more complete a story marketers tell in their commercials, the higher it performs in the rating polls, and the more people like it and want to view it and share it."

That's why you want to tell great stories that people relate to and share. The more that happens, the quicker your movement will get rolling.

How to Craft a Story

Stories have structure. While there are many from which to choose, the structure of a story is predictable. Donald Miller, author of *Story Brand* and *How to Tell a Story*, explains, "A series of random events becomes a story when it's organized and told through a structured plot." He adds, "And it's not always the 'best' stories that get the most attention—it's more often the ones that are the most clearly told. Remember, the human brain is drawn to clarity more than action or comedy."

Miller uses a plot structure for telling stories that has been used thousands of times in movies that earned billions of dollars. Here's the simple plot line: A character has a problem, then meets a guide who gives them a plan and calls them to action. That action either results in a success or failure. This plot line is structured on what American professor of literature Joseph Campbell called "the Hero's Journey."

To entice anyone to change, your stories of failure need to demonstrate to your reader the dire consequences of continuing to do things in a certain way. Your success stories must illustrate how doing something different changes the results achieved. In most cases, your story of failure leads to the problem you encountered. You then learn something that helps you solve the problem successfully, and you share that information. (In doing so, you become the guide.)

In all cases, as the hero goes on his journey, he undergoes inner and outer transformation at each stage. While some descriptions of the Hero's Journey include as many as 12 steps, I like Miller's six-step version, which is easy to understand and apply:

1. A Character
2. Who has a problem
3. Meets a guide who understands their fear
4. And gives them a plan
5. That calls them to action
6. That results in success

To apply one of your stories to this plot model, answer the questions below in your journal. Then, plot them into Miller's six-part structure above.

- At the beginning of your story, what did you want? What were you like?
- What problem or challenge did you have?
- How or from whom did you get help to solve the problem?
- What plan did you create after getting help?
- How did you act on your plan?

- What was at stake? If you failed, what would you have lost?
- How did your story end? What was the transformative or happy result (or the opposite)? How had you changed?

Let's look at how you could apply your answers to Miller's six-part plot structure and create a story. I'll use an example from my life.

1. When I was in high school, I loved reading novels and wanted to pursue a career as a novelist. (Character)
2. My mother told me that only "good writers" could make a living in that manner. I decided that she meant I was not a good enough writer to become a successful novelist. (Problem)
3. Still interested in writing, I signed up for a journalism class taught by a charismatic teacher. (Guide)
4. The teacher encouraged me to write for publications and explained that journalism—specifically magazine journalism—was a career that could pay my bills. He suggested I explore college or university magazine journalism programs. (Plan)
5. I applied to several good journalism programs and was accepted at a few. I chose one to enter. (Action)
6. I graduated four years later with a magazine journalism degree and a month later began working as an editor on a regional publication. I worked and wrote for a variety of publications on a full-time or freelance basis for several years before I decided to apply what I learned to editing nonfiction books. I then wrote a book of my own and became a published nonfiction author. (Success)

You can share your stories in videos, podcasts, articles, blog posts, speeches, media appearances, and books. With every telling, your audience knows you better. When they know, like, and trust you, they become fans as well as eager participants in your movement.

Plus, telling personal stories is a way to be the message and the messenger.

How to Excavate Your Brand Stories

As part of your branding efforts, it's important to dig deep and discover the stories that most effectively promote your message and lead people to your movement. These powerful stories must illustrate the focus of your book, its purpose (and yours), and the transformation you desire. The right stories illustrate the pain and struggle you experienced—and that your audience shares—as well as your ability to overcome them. Or they discuss universal pain points or current issues that affect you and your audience—and lead to prescriptions that alleviate pain or provide solutions with broad implications. The stories you share can also be those of your clients, patients, or customers, but personal stories have more impact. When your stories move from aspiration to struggle to success—and demonstrate how your audience can thrive—people will join your movement in droves.

The stories you tell repeatedly are your "signature stories." Unpack your deepest experiences and tie them to your book and purpose. In your journal, make a list of the stories you could tell. Give each story a title or tag, and then describe the point it makes. For example, if I wanted to illustrate the reason why I desire to start a movement involving people writing for change, I might talk about the books that inspired me to change and impacted my life, such as those written by Richard Bach, Wayne Dyer, and Greg Braden. I'd tag the story "life-changing books" and indicate that it would describe "the life-changing power of a book."

Duplicate the chart below in your journal to create your list of stories. Identify at least three stories.

Story Title or Tag	Point of Story or How it Illustrates Your Mission

Then, use Miller's plot structure to craft a complete story; or learn more about the Hero's Journey and apply it to your narratives.

Your job as a change agent is to dig deep and uncover as many signature stories as possible that emotionally demonstrate the turning points in your life—the ones that transformed you into who you are today. While this exercise isn't always easy and introspection can dredge up old emotions, the payoff is huge. Not only will you change in the process, but you'll be able to deliver your message in a relatable manner that inspires your audience to feel change is possible.

If you struggle to find personal stories to illustrate your message, look outside yourself. Find shining examples of successful change in other people. These stories can inspire your audience as well. And continue delving into the experiences of your own life to find signature stories. Even if you only find one and combine it with those about other people, your message will have more impact.

As you search for your stories, be courageous. It's okay—better than okay—to admit your faults, failures, and struggles. Your transparency will help your audience believe and connect with you.

Share your stories often, both in written and spoken form.

Five Ways to Enhance Your Author Brand

Here are a few more useful strategies for enhancing your brand.

1. *Be authentic*—I'm repeating this point because it's amazing how quickly you can establish a brand simply by being authentic. This is especially true when you are the brand—not your company, book, or service. In the case of authorship and books, the brand tends to be about you, your purpose, and the result you want to achieve. Create a brand around who you are and what you and your book stand for—not something or someone you think the audience will like better. It's vital to be perceived as genuine and as a real person. People naturally take up your cause when they know who you are and what you represent.

2. *Be a Leader*—You may not perceive yourself as a leader, but the fact that you want to author change makes you one. Even before you have followers, show up as a leader, and you will more easily attract people to your movement. As an Author of Change, readers (even potential readers) are the team you lead. They look to you for direction. The success or

failure of your cause is a shared responsibility. Part of your branding relies on a clear definition of what success means to you, to those who choose to read your book, and to the people who join your cause. How you lead them to success becomes part of your brand.

3. *Be confident*—People are attracted to those who demonstrate confidence. Your branding relies on your demonstration of belief in your movement. If you feel uncertain, encounter a setback, or come upon a challenge at any point, be transparent about your struggle. Always communicate your values boldly and rely on personal experiences that make you the expert on your type of change. Remain steadfast in your values and belief in your ability to achieve the desired outcome.

4. *Be consistent*—Consistency is key. Whether it's how you dress or speak, the message you share, the values you demonstrate, or the headshot you use, always be consistent. When you waver, you create a question in your audience's mind about who you are and what you stand for.

5. *Be unique*—Some of the most memorable personal brands are created by enormously unique people. Look at the music industry, for instance—Taylor Swift, Pink!, Ed Sheeran, Bruno Mars, Lady Gaga, Bad Bunny, and Lizzo. Beyond your brand of change, you need to be memorable. Seth Godin, marketer, entrepreneur, speaker, and bestselling author of twenty-one books, including his newest, *This is Strategy*, is known for his glasses and his extremely short blog posts. (His books are short, too.) Mark Twain, a typesetter turned great American novelist, wore white suits year-round, breaking fashion conventions to stand out in a crowd. Rachel Hollis, the bestselling author of *Girl, Wash Your Face* and *Girl, Stop Apologizing* is known as a lifestyle expert with a tell-it-like-it-is communication style and a casual-yet-trendy fashion sense.

I know branding can seem overwhelming, but it is doable—even if you aren't a branding expert or don't choose to hire one. Let me tell you about my process.

It took me about two years to settle on a brand and a brand message: *The Inspiration to Creation Coach*—"With Nina, you **A**chieve **M**ore **I**nspired **R**esults." My friend Karen Stone took me through an exercise that involved a poster board sectioned into four quadrants. She asked a specific question for each one, and I wrote down words related to the question. I then circled the words that spoke to me or showed up more than once. When I had something I thought worked, I took it to my media coach at the time, the late Michael Dresser of the *Dresser After Dark* radio show. He said, "That's not it. Ask everyone you know what you do for them." So I did.

Whether I asked a friend, a colleague, a client, or a reader, the answer was the same: "You inspire me." Got it! *Inspiration* needed to be in my brand message.

Then I looked at the work I was doing in the world—or wanted to do. Everything involved some sort of creation. On my nonfiction writing blog, *Write Nonfiction NOW!*, I inspired aspiring nonfiction writers to create careers as freelance writers and authors and to make a positive and meaningful difference with their words. On my blogging site, *How to Blog a Book*, I inspired bloggers and writers to build a platform, make a difference with their posts, and become authors. And on my main site, NinaAmir.com, I inspired people to create their best selves, best lives, and desires. Boom! *Creation* was a word that needed to be in my brand message.

And that's how the Inspiration to Creation Coach moniker was born. I clearly saw that what I was doing—and wanted to continue doing —was to inspire people to create. And Dresser, along with another media coach, Annie Jennings, gave the brand their blessing.

The use of my last name as an acronym came later. I was attending a National Speakers Association meeting in Northern California and had the good fortune of hearing executive speech coach and sales presentation expert Patricia Fripp speak. She mentioned that she sometimes used her name as an acronym: *Frequently Reinforce Ideas that are Productive and Profitable.* Five minutes later, I had mine: *Achieve More Inspired Results.*

Before commissioning my logo creation, I thought about colors and fonts. I wanted a font that portrayed me as creative and colors that represented me well. (A quick dive into color psychology will help you understand and choose appropriate colors.) I chose purple—imagination and spirituality—and indigo—intuition, perception, consciousness, and service. You can find these colors on Nina Amir.com.

I work with many writers, experts, and bloggers to help them build career plans. Part of this involves branding—although I am not a branding expert. I suggest they think about the themes that run through all their work. When they find a thread that holds everything together, that's the foundation for building their brand. Maybe your theme is nature, consciousness, yoga, relationships, healthy living, safety, spirituality, or LGBTQ+ rights. Use that as a starting point as you build your brand.

Remember you are creating a brand for a book, a movement, and yourself. Also, keep in mind that it's best to have a brand that encompasses the scope of all your book projects, including those you want to produce in the future. Think big. Look beyond this moment. Try to create a brand that serves you and your contribution over time.

More than anything, live your message authentically. Walk your talk. Be a demonstration of change, and your movement will grow organically.

PART TWO
HOW TO INSPIRE CHANGE

6

BUILD ENGAGED PLATFORMS
AND COMMUNITIES

How do you build a tribe? Let me suggest four ways: 1. Discover your passion. Marketing is the act of sharing what you are passionate about. Nothing more. Nothing less... 2. Volunteer to lead. This is everything. Without a leader, you don't have a tribe. You only have a crowd. Marketing is really about leading people who already want to follow. They just need a leader to take them where they already want to go. 3. Be generous. The old marketing was about taking from people. As it turns out, "It is more blessed to give than to receive" is a brilliant marketing strategy. When you lead by serving and by giving, people follow. 4. Provide a way to communicate. People need a way to communicate. They need a way to share their stories.

— MICHAEL HYATT, *PLATFORM: GET NOTICED*
IN A NOISY WORLD

To author change, you must gather a community of like-minded people interested in the type of change you want to inspire. Some aspiring authors think they can do this after their books are published, but that's a mistake. Some think they don't have to do it at all, which is a bigger error. In fact, you need to start building community long before the book goes on sale. Better yet, start the moment you decide to become an author.

This section might seem off track or as if I have gone off on a tangent, since this book promises to teach you how to write a book that changes the world—or lives, communities, and organizations. It's not primarily about building an audience for your book or marketing and promoting it. Therefore, you might think, "I don't need to read these three chapters. I'll skip ahead to the next section, which teaches me how to write my transformational book." Please, don't do that!

The information provided in this section on how to create a community or audience ready to join your movement, buy your book, and act on the change you propose is essential to your success and your book's success. Community building is often overlooked—or ignored —by aspiring Authors of Change, much to the detriment of their desire to make a positive and meaningful difference with their words.

More than other types of authors, as an Author of Change, you need to surround yourself with people who are either aligned with your mission or want and need the transformation you know how to achieve. Without engaged platforms and communities, when your book is published, few people (if any) will be waiting to buy and read your book or to implement the changes it suggests. If you are willing and eager to write and publish your change-inspiring book, embrace community building, too. Even a great book may reach few people if the author doesn't take the time to develop an audience for that book.

Creating change is your goal, and your change-inspiring book is a tool used to achieve that result. When you commit to your purpose and your book's purpose, your community building efforts align with and help you accomplish that purpose. They become another way to share your message, gain support for your cause, and ultimately author change.

You may have heard the words "tribe" or "following," both of which refer to your community. In the publishing world, your community is called your "author platform." An author platform is a built-in readership for your book in your target market. It also equates to your influence with your audience, which is the sum of your visibility within your community, how far your message reaches beyond your current audience, and the amount of authority you are perceived to have with your audience. You can create an author platform in a variety of ways, including writing for publications, blogging, speaking, posting YouTube videos, podcasting, providing online or in-person classes and events, or publishing books. But platforms are not built overnight, and today they need to be larger and stronger than ever before.

A traditional publisher or a literary agent evaluates your platform to determine the potential you, the author, have to sell books. Acquisition editors, who purchase manuscripts for publishing houses, use platform size as part of a formula that determines how much of an advance on sales the publisher will offer for the purchase of your manuscript. Such decisions are based on the value and uniqueness of your book and on your ability to get the book into readers' hands. That task depends in large part on your author platform.

Your platform is measurable in many ways, including the number of followers you have on social media, the number and size of your speaking engagements, the frequency of your radio, podcast, and television appearances, and the number of visitors to your website, viewers of your YouTube station, and/or listeners to your podcast. Platform size is assessed by calculating how many people know who you are and want to hear or read what you have to say. The resulting number quantifies your potential to make money from book sales. Publishers want to sell enough books to earn back the advance paid to you and begin making a profit. If you self-publish, make the same calculation to determine your ability to sell enough books to recover your investment.

Of course, the size of your author platform also indicates your ability to author change. Even a small platform means people who know and follow you are paying attention and should be ready and willing to purchase your book and sign onto your cause.

Too many aspiring authors resist this part of the publishing process. They simply do not want to spend time on marketing or promotion, and platform building involves doing both in the early stages of a book project. But to write a book that can change lives or the world, this step is essential. You must promote your book idea or movement —and even yourself—to potential book buyers. It's true, you don't yet have a product to sell, but you do have a message to share. And that's the crux of platform building—sharing your message with people who might later purchase your book and change personally or change the world. Get your ideal audience on board with your cause, and encourage them to join your movement or become part of your community both online and in the world. Later, tell them about your book.

Aspiring authors often refuse to get involved in platform building for other reasons. For instance, sometimes they don't want to waste time on sites like Bluesky and Instagram, believing they will decrease their available writing time, or feel they will lose privacy by joining social networks. The job of marketing and promotion is considered a business task; some writers don't believe business naturally accompanies creativity (writing) or service (activism). Yet building an author platform is essential for the success of your book. Without a community of like-minded people, any marketing done after the book is published becomes less effective. You want people gathered eagerly around you when you announce the publication of your book —people who know, like, and trust you and your recommendations.

Imagine walking into a room filled with a thousand or more people who applaud as you take the stage. See them listening attentively as you speak and cheering when you tell them your book is available... and for sale at the back of the room. See them quickly heading to the table filled with copies of your book and lining up to a purchase a signed copy. That's a well-developed author platform at work.

Imagine publishing a blog or social media post announcing the release of your book. An hour later, you click on your Author Central account at Amazon.com and see that your book has reached the Amazon Top 100 list in its category! You check back two hours later, and it's reached the #1 spot in its category. That's the power of an author platform.

You can publish your book without building such a platform. However, you'll find it harder to sell your book or convince people to read it. You'll be forced to market to "cold traffic"—to run ads to people who have never heard of you, which is a tough way to approach book marketing. The easier way involves marketing to "warm leads"—people with whom you've already come into contact. Create community now to ensure your audience is ready and waiting when your book is released.

You will find it easier to get involved in platform-building activities when you:

1. Change the terminology from platform building or marketing to "community building." Consider your audience a community of like-minded people who have chosen to interact with you and want to learn more about your subject and make related changes.
2. Shift your focus from selling books to fulfilling your purpose and the purpose of your book—to being of service.

Building a platform feels impersonal and businesslike. Attracting a community of people who want to engage and work with you toward a shared goal has a warmer and fuzzier feel.

Visualize this: You create a Facebook or LinkedIn group related to your cause. You share the group link with your current followers on social media platforms and on your email list. In less than a month, your group gains five hundred members and becomes a community. The members chat with each other and comment on and share your posts, and before you know it, you have a thousand members. Every time you share something related to your mission and purpose, the community members comment, apply your suggestions, and report on their results. They excitedly share your information and the transformation they have experienced with *their* audiences, and before long, your membership quadruples. You now have a large, engaged community.

An engaged community consists of people who don't just read your posts and then leave but who "like," share, and comment on them. This helps your messages gain reach because many social media sites reward popular posts with increased visibility. If you share a link to a blog post on social media, the more shares and click-throughs that social post gets, the more likely it is that Google will move your website up in the search engine results pages, which makes it more easily found in searches. When your message is seen often and is easily found, you sell books more effectively because people are already interested and involved in your cause and are talking about it on social media.

Earning money from book sales is important, and the income can help sustain your movement. But most Authors of Change want to be of service and make a difference first and foremost. Sell books to readers so you can fulfill your purpose and that of your book. With that focus in mind, marketing tasks become more palatable. After all, you want people to read your book and create change in themselves, their organizations, or the world. That happens when they purchase the book and act on the information between its covers. Each time someone buys, reads, and acts on your book's content, you fulfill your purpose, and so does your book. Marketing then becomes key to fulfilling the purpose you have in mind for you and your book. Not only that, but all your community building activities also fall into the realm of contribution in the sense of being of service to others.

You wouldn't be writing your book if you didn't want to serve in some way—to help people have more faith, go on a healing journey, or become female leaders. You may want to be an author to encourage bipartisanship in politics, reduce global warming, or encourage boys to dance. Your book is your way of contributing, and everything you do to market yourself and your book revolves around your aspiration to be of service.

Your marketing and promotion efforts, including those meant to build an engaged community, need not be heavy-handed sales pitches. Instead, make them service oriented. For example, you can write blog posts that offer tips and strategies for implementing change. Your updates on social networks can consist of quote posts that inspire people to take a specific action. Your weekly email can provide subscribers with your latest updates, as well as news from around the world related to your cause and suggestions on how to respond to new developments. As a further example, you can build your mailing list by offering a free PDF that provides those who opt in to your email list to receive, say, twenty tips on how to implement change immediately. In your LinkedIn group, you can share news articles, tips, strategies, success stories, or your own experiences implementing change.

None of this has anything to do with marketing per se. It's about service and contributing value to your audience—but it builds your community in the process. You might even include some of this information in more depth in your book.

Build Community Now—Not Later

Marketing expert Seth Godin says you need to begin building your community several years prior to releasing a book. From my experience working on my own platform and watching clients and colleagues build theirs, I suggest you start when you get the idea for a book—if not earlier. That's the time to start engaging with and gathering your potential audience.

Share your message and your purpose on a grassroots level. Then, people get excited about the change you want to create and eagerly join your cause. Speak, write articles, pursue traditional media appearances, blog, be active on social media sites, podcast, vlog, produce webinars and teleseminars, publish videos, and host virtual and physical events. Anything you do that gets your name and message in front of your ideal audience helps build community.

Too many aspiring authors wait to build community until they feel they are good enough speakers, are comfortable on video, know how to write a blog post, or understand social media. You will never do all these things perfectly. And there will never be a perfect time to get started. Go back and look at early videos of people you respect. Read their first blog posts. You'll notice something important: They started even when they weren't ready, and they improved as they continued to share their messages. Follow in their footsteps. Start where you are and grow from there.

As you do so, focus on the fact that you are inviting like-minded people to your community—people with whom you would enjoy interacting. This helps the process become one you enjoy. In an interview for *Darling Magazine*, Seth Godin said, "[Revolution] only happens from a small group of people, and it's totally possible. We need to understand where the needle is if we want to move it. Where the needle is in one simple sentence: 'People like me do things like this.' What I mean by that is, if you went to Bareilly, India, it would never occur to you to wear stiletto heels because you're surrounded by people who would laugh at you. So, the people in Bareilly say to themselves, 'People like me, we dress like this!'"

Your community will have a culture, which according to Godin, "is which group we think we're a part of and how we think that group behaves in a situation 'like this.'" Be the voice of "people like us" and remind your audience in your own words, "People like us do this; we don't do that.'" This is a statement of values, not of right or wrong.

To create an engaged community around your cause, it's imperative that your potential audience understand you are like them. Don't put yourself above your readers; put yourself in the community with them. It's true, you will become their leader, but you won't be different than them. You want the same things. You've struggled with similar issues. You share their aspirations. (Remember: *Be the message and the messenger.*)

I often tell my audience, "I'm an everywoman—someone who is facing or has experienced the same challenges you face. I discovered a few things that worked for me, and I want to share them with you. Maybe they'll work for you, too. At the very least, they will provide you with a starting place to discover what does work for you." This positions me as part of the community with a desire to be of service and share what I know, and people connect with that.

Know Your Audience

All this talk about community raises an important question: What type of people do you want in your community? In the publishing world, your community equates to your target audience, also called your market; and you may have heard how important it is to know your reader. Marketers tell you to create a customer avatar, which is a fictional character that represents your ideal reader. Indeed, a community member or reader profile helps you understand the motivating beliefs, fears, and desires that influence their buying or reading decisions and their actions. Such a profile helps you turn a somewhat amorphous idea about who you are writing for into a character as real to you as a living human being. You can even make up a name for this avatar. This clear picture of your ideal reader makes it easier to write your book and know who to attract into your community.

Take a moment to consider what type of people you want in your community. Keep in mind that these are the same people who will want to read your book and take on the change you propose. In your journal, make a list of the characteristics shared by the people who will read your book—your ideal readers—and join your movement. Include the following traits:

3. **Interests, goals, and values**—What are they interested in? (For example: personal development, family, activism, spirituality, or community service.) To identify this characteristic of your ideal reader and community member, you can complete this sentence: *My ideal reader is interested in...* And what are their goals and values? Complete these sentences: *My ideal reader aspires to... wants to... would like to achieve... My ideal reader values...*

4. **Favorite media sources, scenes, and activities**—What types of things do your ideal readers do and what places do they frequent? (Example: Tedx events, sports bars, the International Conference on Green Energy, the International Conference on Spirituality and Psychology, Michael Hyatt's Facebook page, political rallies, the *Free the People* blog, or *Yes! Magazine*.) To identify this characteristic, complete sentences like: *My ideal reader would read [BOOK TITLE]... My ideal reader would subscribe to [MAGAZINE, BLOG or PERIODICAL]... My ideal reader would attend [CONFERENCE or EVENT]... My ideal reader would frequent this [WEBSITE, SOCIAL MEDIA PAGE or GROUP]...*

5. **Demographics**—What is your target reader's age, gender, location, profession (and title), marital status, number of children, and annual income? (Example: My reader is between the ages of 50 and 75, female, in the US, a former stay-at-home mom, still married, has two or three grown children, and earns $100,000 per year.)

6. **Favorite Quote**—What quote would they share or feel most resonates with their beliefs? (Example: "Never doubt that a small group of thoughtful, committed, citizens can change the world. Indeed, it is the only thing that ever has." —Margaret Mead) Finding a quote provides a powerful way to understand your target reader better, effectively getting inside their heads.

7. **Aspirational Challenges**—What challenges related to his or her goals does your ideal reader struggle with? (For example: finding a way to lead effectively while scaling a business, discovering strategies to become a better stepparent, reducing stress to become healthier, feeling connected to God after loss, or creating a more connected primary relationship.) This information allows you to write a book that addresses your reader's aspirations and helps them move through obstacles experienced on the way to achieving that goal.

8. **Pain Points**—What are your ideal reader's most deep-seated and painful difficulties that relate to the topic of your book? (For example: *I'm afraid of losing essential employees if I can't lead well; I'll never get married and will be lonely my entire life; I believe I haven't had a positive effect on my stepchildren; I am so stressed and worry that stress will make me too sick to provide for my family;* or *my marriage is failing and I believe I need to get a divorce.*) This information motivates your readers. If you promise to help them get out of pain, they are likely to take action.

9. **Objections**—What would make this person decide *not* to buy your book, join your cause, or take a new and different action? (For example: *I don't have time*; *I might fail*; *nothing I do will make a difference*; *it's too expensive*; or *it will take too much time.*) Reduce their objections, and you increase your chances to gain readers and community members.

10. **Questions**—What information does your ideal reader need to feel confident taking action? What questions are they asking? (For example: *How fast can I expect results? Who has succeeded? Will it be hard? How much will it cost? How much time will it take?*) Knowing their questions allows you to answer them, which helps your ideal reader decide to purchase, read, take action, or join your cause.

When the time arrives to create a business plan or book proposal, you must identify your market(s). Knowing your ideal reader provides the foundation for that work. Additionally, knowing where to find your ideal reader helps you know where to connect with potential community members and readers. With that knowledge, you can also create a marketing plan. Go back and reread your book's purpose (see Chapter 2) and determine if you have accurately described your target reader.

A deep understanding of your reader makes a huge difference in your ability to write a book that moves readers to action. When I began writing this book, I had a picture of my ideal reader that wasn't as broad as it needed to be. Once I got clarity on my customer avatar, I was able to produce the manuscript faster and write for my reader— you.

How to Build an Engaged Community

In the past, marketing used a "push" model: The more you pushed out your message or brand to your audience, the more engagement and name recognition you achieved, and that encouraged people to buy something from you. Today, you still need name recognition and engagement, but it's achieved more effectively by "pulling" people to you with valuable content provided on a consistent basis. "Pull" marking is often called content marketing because it involves the creation of blog posts, social media updates, videos, and other content you share with your potential audience, which then pulls them toward you. The more of your content they see, the more interested they become in learning more about you. The continual stream of valuable content works like a magnet, drawing them to your website, cause, or book.

Think about a time when you have frequently seen posts from an expert sharing information on a topic of interest in your Instagram or LinkedIn feed. Eventually, you clicked through to read the content shared. You may even have opted in to receive a free book or paid for a program. Perhaps you recall a television commercial that shared information and tips on a problem with which you struggle. After seeing it a few times, you pulled out your computer and conducted an online search to find the company and read more about it. In both examples, you were pulled toward the company or person because you repeatedly saw their content. However, the marketing didn't have a "buy now" message; it took a "here's some valuable information" approach.

Marketing research shows that it takes at least eight "touches" before someone purchases from you. That's why it's so important to provide a continuous stream of valuable content to potential readers.

As you create content, focus on your community members' wants and needs—not yours. Your potential readers are tuned into station WIIFM ('What's In It For Me?'). They want to know what benefit they get out of following you, joining your movement, buying your book, or taking on your brand of change. If your message revolves around you, they'll lose interest quickly. If your message focuses on them, you'll get their attention and gain their trust.

Here's a list of the ways you can share your message and build your community:

- Publish and share blog posts
- Write guest blog posts for other bloggers
- Get interviewed on podcast shows
- Speak on radio shows
- Appear on television shows
- Build your mailing list
- Share online press releases
- Blog your book (Read *How to Blog a Book* to find out how)
- Conduct free teleseminars
- Offer free webinars
- Speak to groups or at conferences
- Write articles for publications
- Hold live (or virtual) workshops
- Create live or recorded videos and share them on Bluesky, YouTube, or Instagram

11. Start a group on social media
12. Develop a presence on one or more social media sites
13. Join and get involved with organizations, associations, and other groups

With this list fresh in your mind, evaluate your degree of willingness or ability to take on some of these community building activities. Answer the following set of questions in your journal.

Ten Questions About Your Current Community

- Do you see yourself as an extrovert or an introvert?
- If you are an extrovert, how do you currently interact with your audience, and how *could* you interact with them? If you are an introvert, what activities or situations might allow you to comfortably share your message with potential readers?
- How often have you shared your message or purpose with others in the past?
- How many people know about your message or purpose at this moment?
- When you have shared your message or purpose, what reaction did you receive? (Have people wanted to get on board? Or did they tell you that you were crazy?)
- How do the people connected with you either online or offline know you? How did you meet or connect?
- To what groups, organizations, or networks do you belong?
- Would you say you have an engaged community now?
- Are you carrying negativity around the task of social networking or other online promotional activities?
- How much time each week do you devote to community building?

Based on your answers to the questions above, journal on these topics:

- When you speak about your message or purpose, do you inspire others? Why do you think you do or don't inspire others? If you don't know, ask friends or colleagues who have heard you speak, read your writing, followed you on social media, and so on. Then journal about how you feel about their comments and what actions you need to take.

- What do you enjoy about being social—online or off? What don't you enjoy? What might help you enjoy it more?
- Do people want to follow you or join your movement? Can you influence them to do so? Why or why not?
- What aspects of community building are least comfortable for you? Why? How could you gain a higher comfort level?
- What aspect of community building is comfortable—and effective—for you right now? How can you use this specific activity to increase your current community size to three, five, or ten times its current size?

If you've begun creating a community around your movement, make a list below of the tools you're using; for example, writing articles for local newspapers, starting a MeetUp group, creating Instagram, Substack, or LinkedIn accounts, and speaking to groups.

1.

2.

3.

4.

5.

6.

7.

8.

9.

10.

Now consider what you could add to your community building tool-box. Think of ways to share your message that might be outside your comfort zone. Look at the list I provided above and choose five additional activities that could help you build community—ones you may have avoided even though you had a strong sense they could work well. Maybe using LinkedIn feels difficult, posting a video to YouTube seems intimidating, or asking people to come to an event seems impossible. Try one. Take a baby step. For example, submit an opinion piece to your local newspaper, set up a Bluesky or LinkedIn account, or go to a MeetUp related to your cause. Make a list below of the activities you will try next:

1.

2.

3.

4.

5.

Use the steps you just completed to build your book's marketing plan. You now know what you have done, what has worked, and what you will try in the future to build your community and sell books.

As you gather a community around you, your book, and your movement, always approach your efforts as if you are speaking to one person—someone you know well and want to serve (like your customer avatar). When I was in journalism school, we were taught that communication has two essential components: a broadcaster and a receiver. You are the broadcaster. Your audience is the receiver. You don't need to be loud or pushy to get heard. You simply need to speak directly to the people in your audience in a manner they can hear and understand. (Recall the information in Chapter 3 about influence and apply it here.)

When people understand your message and connect with it emotionally, they feel inspired to change. Touch people personally and demonstrate that you are bringing resources that meet their needs, and you'll pull them to you. Not only that, enthusiastic community members will also share your message with their friends and followers (their audiences), who in turn will share it with theirs. Word of mouth then becomes your best promotional tool.

It's Never Too Early to Attract a Community

Don't worry about starting to create a community too soon or before you feel 100 percent ready. See your early efforts as test marketing for your book concept and cause. As you share your message, you'll have many opportunities to clarify your purpose, mission, and signature stories. Start sharing these early in the process to evaluate audience response. Determine if you are inspiring change. Check if your message resonates with your target market; tweak and hone it, then test again. When people respond in the way you desire—taking action by joining your community, sharing your content, or creating change on some level—release your book. And be sure you've used this feedback to perfect the book's manuscript before publication.

Expecting a book to build community represents backward thinking no matter how you publish. A publisher or literary agent won't want to build your career for you; they want to capitalize on and support what you've built for yourself. It's no different if you self-publish. The platform you create prior to your book release launches the book. In either case, the book then increases your community's growth potential.

A community interested in your movement becomes your fans, followers, and supporters as well as the adopters of your brand of change. They become your living advertisements for transformation, and as advocates for your message, serve as a volunteer sales force.

Platform building equates to reaching more people with your message, and as a result, selling more books, impacting more individuals, and creating more transformation. That's the bottom line. If you feel reluctant to market and promote your book, your message, or your purpose, remember your efforts draw to you a group of people interested in becoming part of your movement. Building community helps you to reach readers and effect change on a larger scale. Focus on gathering a large group of like-minded people and serving them to the best of your ability. That's when building an audience becomes easier, more enjoyable, and better aligned with your mission, allowing you to inspire and motivate change.

7
MAKE A DIFFERENCE ONLINE

"I am only one, but I am one. I cannot do everything, but I can do something. And I will not let what I cannot do interfere with what I can do."

— EDWARD EVERETT HALE

The Internet provides amazing opportunities to inspire change. As a savvy Author of Change, put this powerful tool to use to reach potential readers and members of your movement before, during, and after you write and publish your book. The more change you inspire online, the higher the likelihood your book will ride the wave of interest—and results—you create.

As of October, 2024, 5.52 billion people worldwide, or 67.5 percent of the global population, enjoyed Internet access, and the number of Internet users grows annually. By tapping into the power of online tools, you can reach your target audience and gather an engaged community more effectively than ever before. The Internet allows you to reach a worldwide audience, so don't dismiss it.

According to Statista, people around the globe spent an average of two hours and twenty minutes per day using social media in 2024. That amounts to 36.5 days per year—almost an entire work week spent online. It's no wonder many people balk at using social media; it can become an addiction and a time suck. However, time online proves enormously effective and productive for writers and change agents, especially if you employ a strategy that allows you enough time to write and to support your movement.

While some writers adopt a single-social-media-site approach to building an online readership—perhaps as their way of limiting their time spent online—in my opinion, that's a mistake. What if you decided to use Google Plus, for example, as your primary social media site and then Google decided to shut the site down, which happened in 2019? All the work you did to create a community there would be lost. The same would be true if the one social media site you use most gets banned in your country, goes bankrupt, or disappears for any other reason.

Additionally, a one-social-media-site strategy means you, your book, and your movement can only be found by the users of that specific site. As a result, you limit the number of potential readers you can draw to you and the number of people who engage with and share your work. Plus, other sites might attract more users who fall into your target market. By failing to have a presence on those other sites, you effectively cut off your ability to reach that audience.

I'm not saying you need to be involved in every social media site. I am suggesting you try several social media sites and online tools to determine which ones work best for you. As you test different social networks, you'll also discover which sites are most effective for reaching your specific audience. Additionally, you'll find sites that allow you to express your message in your unique way and to enjoy the process of online community building. For instance, if you love taking photos, you'll enjoy Instagram. If you like creating long posts

—almost like a blog post—you might prefer Facebook or LinkedIn. If you prefer everything to be visual, Pinterest might be the place for you. And if short-form updates and a constant flow of information turn you on, X or Bluesky might be your ticket.

Almost every segment of the world population uses social media, including your target market. A June 2023 report by the Pew Research Center indicated that many activists, for example, are politically engaged on social media. According to the report, "About one-third of social media users (34 percent) say they have taken part in a group that shares an interest in an issue or cause, while a smaller share (26 percent) say they have encouraged others to take action on social media in the past year." Additionally, 14 percent have looked up information on protests or rallies happening in their area, 14 percent changed their profile picture to support a cause, and 12 percent used hashtags related to a political or social issue during the previous year. Altogether, 46 percent of social media users said they had performed at least one of these activities in the previous year.

As with almost every subject or movement, you can find your audience by searching on related hashtags. For example, if your purpose involves consciousness or spirituality, search #biblestudy, #prayer, #spirituality, #meditation, or #consciousness to find your tribe. Doing these types of searches also helps you discover groups related to your cause. Of course, you can always start your own group or create a new hashtag, but utilizing ones already in use—especially those used most by your target market—will attract people interested in your topic.

You may find that generalized social networking sites, such as Bluesky or Instagram, aren't as useful as those specific to your subject area. For instance, if you travel the world writing about environmental change, and your book is on this topic as well, Instagram might be a fabulous site to share photos and gather a community. However, you might attract more followers on a site like Care2.com, which focuses on green issues, good causes, ethical organizations, fair trade, and other charitable issues. Research social networks specific to your cause or the transformation you want to create. Good examples of topic-specific social media sites include SelfGrowth.com (covering topics related to spirituality and personal development), HumanityHealing.org (focused on making the world a better place), and Happiness.com (dedicated to mutual support, compassion, and self-improvement, as well as enhancing personal growth and happiness and living a life of authenticity and joy). Or explore the multitude of groups on Facebook and LinkedIn or Threads on Instagram that cover related topics, then join the one(s) that seems to attract people in your target market.

The youth of the world understand the power of the Internet. Raised on technology and social media, when they want to share anything at all, they whip out their phones, create a video or photo, and immediately share it online. Just look at the clips taken by the students during the Marjory Stoneman Douglas High school shooting in Parkland, Florida. It was innate to them to take video while shots were being fired in their classrooms and gunmen paraded in front of them—and to upload those gruesome videos live to Snapchat. In this way, the nation got a disturbing peek into the horrifying reality of a mass shooting as it occurred. Of course, these videos quickly went viral on Facebook, as did real-time tweets about the shooting.

Today, social media posts have become standard operating procedure when responding to any event, no matter the issue or your age. In August, 2019, when *Good Morning America* host Lara Spencer joked about Britain's young Prince George taking ballet, the dance community rallied to support him and other boys who dance—all via social media. At issue was the bullying and shaming of young male dancers. Professional dancers, celebrities, dance-related companies, and parents of dancing boys posted for days—until *Good Morning America* ran a segment that included an apology.

Video has more power than almost any other online tool. In fact, live video often has more power than prerecorded video. If you want to see what kind of impact you can have with this medium, look up videos about elephant poaching or horse slaughter. Look up Al Gore's videos related to environmentalism or the melting of polar icecaps. Check out the video of Frank Stephens, an actor with Down's Syndrome, speaking to the UN about the value of his life. Or watch the replay of the eighteen-year-old grandson of Holocaust survivors demanding climate action from Democrats. Like theirs, your videos and status updates might go viral.

Choose Your Social Media Channels

If you are reticent to go online to build community, remind yourself why you need to build a network of people interested in your cause, mission, or book. Then, pick one social media site to begin. Use it as your primary channel for sharing your message. You can expand to other channels after you get your feet wet. Even if you choose to have a presence on more than one social media channel, you likely will discover one channel you enjoy that your audience likes, too.

Choose your main channel carefully. You want a presence on a social networking site that provides the most potential readers or followers. Research where your audience hangs out online. Every year, new studies help identify the right site for any target market. For instance, check out data and infographics provided by SproutSocial.com, Pewresearch.org, Hootsuite.com, or Khoros.com. A quick online search yields abundant demographic information.

Pew Research provided this data in November 2024:

Who uses each social media platform?

Usage of the major online platforms varies by factors such as age, gender, and level of formal education.

% of U.S. adults who say they ever use _ by ...

	Ages 18–29	30–49	50–64	65+
Facebook	68	78	70	59
Instagram	76	66	36	19
LinkedIn	40	41	30	15
X (Formerly Twitter)	38	25	15	8
Pinterest	43	43	33	22
Snapchat	65	32	14	4
YouTube	93	94	86	65
WhatsApp	30	40	28	18
Reddit	46	35	11	4
TikTok	59	40	26	10
BeReal	10	2	1	<1

Note: Respondents who did not give an answer are not shown.
Source: Survey of U.S. adults conducted Feb. 1 – June 10, 2024

This type of research helps you decide which social media sites are right for you, your movement, and your book. Commit to one—or more—and get started. Post often and consistently and stake your claim wherever possible by creating your own online groups. Or demonstrate your expertise by joining and participating in existing groups.

Take a Multichannel Social Media Approach

Once you have chosen a primary social media channel, consider expanding to a multichannel approach to online community building. It is possible to become highly visible on many—if not all—social media sites without spending all your time on the Internet. The strategy is simple: Be active on as many sites as possible, but only spend time on those that best highlight your message or bring you joy.

Let me explain. I'm suggesting that you create accounts on X, Facebook, LinkedIn, Pinterest, and Instagram—the most common and long-lasting sites—and share on them consistently. You can automate such posts if necessary using any number of free or paid social media scheduling tools. However, make the best use of your time by *engaging* consistently (daily or at least weekly) on your primary channel—the site you find most useful or fun. This includes commenting, replying to comments, and sharing other people's content.

This multichannel approach offers many benefits:

- Your potential readers can find you and your work in a variety of places
- Establishes a strong online presence
- Increases your visibility on all social networks
- Builds your platform efficiently

- Provides contexts where you can develop a tribe, either on one site or many sites
- Focuses your online marketing time and energy
- Allows you to spend an amount of time on social media that is acceptable to you

You can appear extremely active on most sites without spending large hunks of time on them. A variety of applications such as Buffer or CoSchedule can help automate the sharing of your content on all of your chosen social media sites. Most sites frown on this practice, but you can do it anyway. For instance, my Instagram account is set up to post to my Facebook page each time I share on that site. I post numerous times per week on most social media channels using a plugin on my blog, and I schedule posts in advance to publish using Buffer.

Some authors choose to spend time on sites that allow advertising, like Facebook, because that makes their content more effective. They share to other sites but put time and money where they can "buy" more views. Advertising on social media sites has become increasingly important as sites change their algorithms on a regular basis. For example, it gets harder all the time to get your message seen on Facebook unless you pay. Even LinkedIn looks for posts with higher engagement and shows them to more users.

One caution: Don't choose a site you'll find difficult to use. For example, if you never take photos with your cell phone, don't choose Instagram as your primary channel. You'll struggle, get discouraged, and eventually give up. Instead, find sites that have less of a learning curve and that you find at least somewhat interesting and enjoyable.

The PBS Approach to Social Media Use

Additionally, you can take American marketing specialist and author Guy Kawasaki's Public Broadcasting System (PBS) approach to social media. During a keynote speech for the <u>New Media Expo</u> in Las Vegas, Nevada, he explained, "I want to have a large following so sporadically I can promote whatever I want to promote." To accomplish that, he is active on a variety of social media networks and does an extremely effective job of both sharing his own content and curating the content of others. Like PBS, he provides great value to his followers 365 days per year—basically ad free. For this "service," Kawasaki feels he "earns" the right to promote his books (or something else) once or twice a year, almost like a telethon. PBS lovers put up with telethons because of the value they get out of the station's programs. And the television station offers premiums in return for a donation, much like the bonuses authors offer to book buyers.

Kawasaki doesn't feel guilty about promoting his books occasionally because all year long he provides his followers with benefit. He works hard to serve his audience, and that builds a network he can use when it's time to market a new book—or the company he evangelizes. In this way, he explained, his fans and followers end up with a sense of reciprocation. "They feel, 'The least I can do is buy Guy's book'" when he asks them to do so.

For anyone who doesn't like the idea of developing an online community for the express purpose of selling books, the PBS approach to social media may be more palatable. It allows you to provide a valuable service and make an occasional offer—"buy my book."

The Station and Satellite Strategy for Online Community Building

No matter which social media sites you choose or the approach you take on those sites, you need an effective social media strategy for sharing content and promoting your cause and book online. I suggest you use what I call the Station and Satellite Strategy. Let me explain.

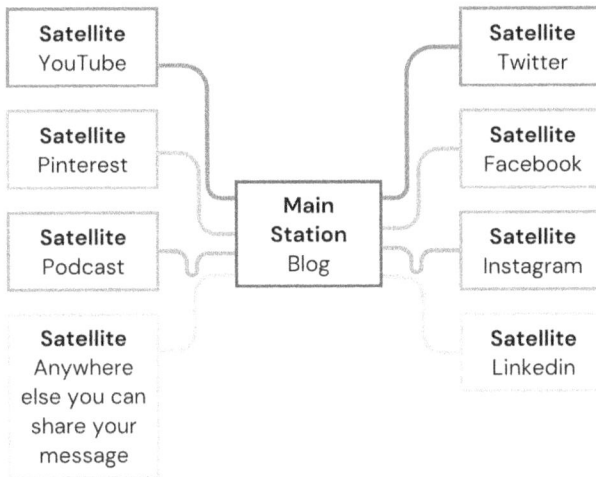

The easiest and most efficient way to build your platform and gain influence and expert status online begins with a blog. Your blog is part of your website, which is the place where you do business, entertain, share valuable information, and attract people to your movement. It's also your main broadcast *station*. From here, you broadcast your message to your *satellites*—social media sites.

Your Station

In the media world, a station is the primary place where information is produced and transmitted. You've likely driven by a radio or television station sporting large satellite dishes. In the building, producers and hosts create shows and share episodes via radio or television waves. You blog serves this same purpose. It's your means for broadcasting info about your book and your mission.

There is little difference between a blog and a website. A website is an online content management system that may or may not feature a blog. A blog is a type of website created with blogging technology, like WordPress. However, the blog is simply a specific type of page on the website.

A blog is regularly updated with new content displayed in reverse chronological order (i.e., with newer posts at the top). Old-style websites without blogs are static—pages are created and then only changed for occasional page or design updates. In this sense, a website without a blog is like a brochure about you, your book, and your business made available in cyberspace. A blog, on the other hand, is dynamic. The site has some brochure-like aspects, such as the home page or 'about' page, but the blog is updated frequently and allows for visitor interaction via comments. Plus, readers can share blog posts to social media sites if the site owner makes this function available to visitors.

Effective blogging requires regular and consistent publication of content that benefits your audience and demonstrates how to create change in ways that line up with your book's suggestions. Each time you publish blog content, you effectively broadcast your message into cyberspace.

It's important not to have an "If you build it, they will come" attitude to your blog, or for that matter, to your book. (Think *Field of Dreams.*) If you consistently publish blog posts several times per week, you will eventually see your site move up in the search engine results pages. That means a search on your topic brings up the URL to your website or to a specific post in the first ten results—that is, in the first page of search engine results. That's because Google indexes new content in a search for keywords. When it identifies keywords often used on your site, it knows to show your site to anyone using those keywords in a search. The more indexed content on your site on one topic—one keyword or keyword phrase—the more "discoverable" you become in related searches. For instance, if you are writing about cleaning up the oceans, Google should find related keywords in your posts, such as oceans, cleanup, ocean cleanup, save the oceans, or any variation. If your book is about improving mental self-talk, use keywords like self-talk, mental chatter, negativity, positivity, and mindset so Google understands your site's focus. Don't stuff your posts full of these keywords, but rather use them naturally in your content.

Your Satellites

Relying on Internet searches to drive new traffic to your site is not sufficient, though, especially when you first begin blogging. You also must put your content in front of those who might be interested. That's where your *satellites* come into play. A satellite is an artificial body placed in orbit around the earth, moon, or another planet to collect information or for communication. Social media sites serve as satellites that orbit your website and blog. Join social media sites to put satellites into orbit and use them to communicate your message beyond your website.

First, broadcast your message to your blog readers by creating blog posts. Second, broadcast this content to your satellite stations—your social media accounts. All you need is a sentence describing your post—or even the title—and a URL to share in a social media update. Or copy and paste the first paragraph or first few paragraphs of the post into the site's new post form. Publish a "status update" on as many social media sites as possible. Include some hashtags to help those searching for your topic find the content. Hashtags are your keywords. Using the examples above, relevant hashtags might include: #oceans, #cleanupoceans, #cleanup, #saveouroceans, and #conservation, or #self-talk, #mentalchatter, #negativity, #positivity, #mindset, #personalgrowth, and #personaldevelopment. (Note that when you use hashtags in a post, in order to be searchable, they must not be immediately followed by commas or any other punctuation.)

Beyond writing posts and sharing that content to social media sites, spend a little time each day checking your satellite stations to engage with fans and followers who have shared or commented on your content. Of course, do the same for those who comment on your blog. (If you are focused solely on one social media site, only take these actions there.)

You can curate content on your social media sites as well, but only do so if it is brand appropriate for your brand. If you read an article or spot a post, social media update, or other information that supports your message and mission, your followers will enjoy it as well and will come to see you as a good source for related content, not just your own. Sharing other experts' content improves your authority in your audience's eyes. Plus, it's a nice thing to do for others who are experts in your chosen field.

Before you continue reading, take a moment to answer in your journal the following questions about community building online. They assume you have a website, use social media, and plan to blog or have begun blogging.

1. Do you enjoy blogging, and how often do you publish posts?
2. Do you share your blog posts to social media sites? If not, why? And if so, how often?
3. Which social networks do you enjoy, use most, and find useful?
4. Do your social media followers engage with you, for example, by leaving comments, tagging you on posts, or sharing your posts?

5. On which social networks do you get the most engagement?

- Twitter/X
- Facebook
- LinkedIn
- Pinterest
- Instagram
- YouTube
- TikTok
- iTunes (podcast)
- Bluesky

6. What holds you back from spending more time or effort engaging about your message and mission with people on social networks?
7. Do you respond to those who mention you on social networks?
8. Do you reach out and connect with other experts or potential followers on social media?
9. Are you a member of any groups or forums on social networks? If yes, how involved are you in them? Do you find them useful, and if so, how?

What to Blog About

You may be wondering what to write about in blog posts. It's simple: Write about topics that relate to and align with your book and your cause. Adopt the mental frame that you want to demonstrate you are an expert with valuable information to share. And you want site visitors to feel the need to return often to read posts, gain information, join your cause, and buy your book. Accomplish these goals by sharing valuable content on your topic of expertise—your brand of change.

What's the most valuable content you have? It's the content in your book. Each of your book's chapters provides material for blog posts. And it is likely you continually learn new things related to your message and cause that also become building blocks for posts.

Consider writing about:

- the foundational principles of your message
- research related to your cause
- case studies that demonstrate your point
- in-depth concepts you've chosen to exclude from your book
- current news related to your message
- topics related to your book
- themes in your book
- interviews with people who have contributed to your movement or have been instrumental in your topic area
- your thoughts on other people's books or new developments in your field
- anything and everything in your book

Don't be afraid of giving away your "best stuff" on your blog. Your readers want your best; in fact, they demand it. That's what keeps them coming back. Also, don't worry about revealing too much of your book's content. While you don't want to share more than 30 percent of your book's content verbatim on your blog (if you plan to traditionally publish), you can share a lot. Look at publishing blog posts on the topic of your book as a way to test-market your concepts. If your audience engages with your posts and joins your cause (by subscribing to your email list or following you on social media), that's proof your book will enjoy the same interest. When it comes time to write the book, you can use some of your blog content, but rewrite and revise the text so it is not deemed "previously published" work. (Although many blogs have been turned into books using primarily published content, these days some publishers frown on previously published work found on a blog.)

Consider developing a plan to guide your blogging efforts and keep your content focused on your book, message, and cause. In your journal, or in a mind mapping program like Freemind, Mind Node, or Mindjet, brainstorm blog post ideas. A mind map is a visual way to brainstorm thoughts around a topic without initially worrying about order and structure. Your mind map is a diagram representing your ideas. Link these ideas together and arrange them around a central concept—in this case, the topic of your book. A mind map looks like this:

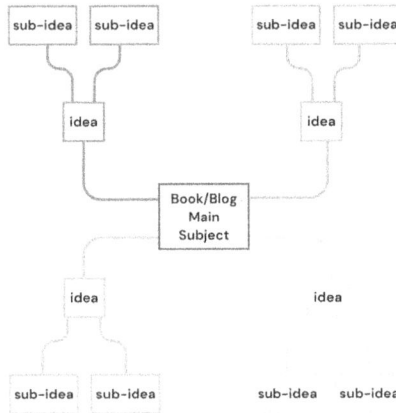

Once you have brainstormed a variety of topics, determine what content to publish on your blog and when. Create a blog schedule, such as publishing a post every Tuesday and Thursday morning at 7 a.m. Then, determine what content you will publish on each of those days.

If you want to write a book about the transformative power of rituals, you might have brainstormed content ideas for your book. Your blog would contain similar content. As you begin the process, your mind map for your book might look like this:

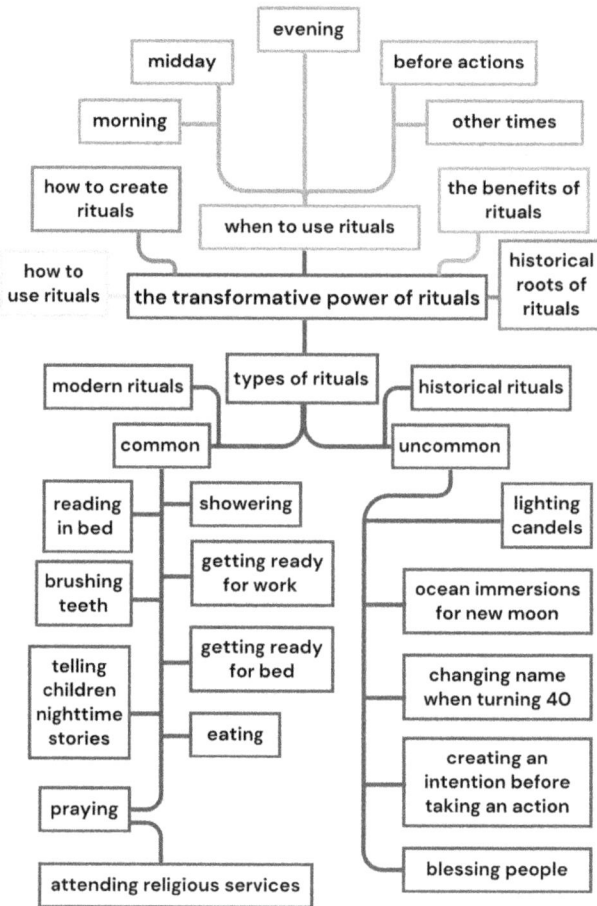

Of course, you would continue to brainstorm until the mind map was totally fleshed out and you'd run out of ideas. Your blog posts would not be identical to your book's content.

Now, use the topics you've developed to create a three-month blog plan, like this:

Recreate the mind map above (either on paper or using an app) and fill in each week with the number of posts you will write per week (one, two, three or more) and each post's title or topic.

Now you are ready to start blogging!

Using Your Blog to Become an Expert

When you publish blog posts regularly and consistently, people perceive you as a subject expert. The more often your content is seen by your target audience, the more they consider you an authority and influencer. If you recall, influence helps you create change. Make the effort to stick to the topic of your book or message on your main station and satellites. Stay on purpose. If you do, over time, you will become known as a thought leader.

For example, when I began blogging my book, *How to Blog a Book*, I was not an expert on the topic. In fact, I had never blogged a book. I had expertise in book writing, publishing, and editing. I had an idea about how to intentionally plan a book, write it, publish it, and promote it online. I tried blogging a book—and I wrote about the process as I carried out my plan. Writing and publishing three or four blog posts per week on the topic of blogging a book made me an expert.

In only five months, you could find my website on the first page of Google search results—in the #1 spot—when you searched for anything related to blogging a book, blog-to-book deals, book blogging, or how to blog a book. I accomplished this by writing about blogging, blogging books, blog-to-book deals, how to blog a book, and blogged books. (Those were my keywords and hashtags.) By doing so, I achieved perceived expert status on the topic. Of course, the process of blogging the book gave me real experience and expertise in the subject area. I've remained the premier expert on blogging books, but I was not an expert before I began that blog.

If you write change-inspiring fiction, you too can use your blog to become an expert. Find the most prevalent themes and subjects in your novels—the ones that run through almost all of your books, then blog about those topics. Consider writing a short work of nonfiction on one or more of those topics as well; this gets you recognized as an authority, especially since the book will come up in an online search.

When readers, clients, customers, journalists, and organizations seeking speakers conduct an Internet search on a particular topic and find you and your blog on the first page of Google search results, they perceive you as an expert. Period. You hardly need to do anything else. Of course, when you publish a book on the same topic as your blog, you seal the deal.

Online Influence Helps You Make a Difference

Using any combination of these strategies—or all of them—helps transform you into a successful blogger, an online influencer, and an authority with the ability to inspire change. Additionally, by using the station-satellite strategy, you set yourself up to sell books. According to a survey of book-buyer influence conducted by the American Booksellers Association, readers decide what books to buy based upon author reputation and personal recommendations.

Readers buy books because they know and trust the author and associate value with that person. Or they make a purchase because someone they know and trust suggests that they do so. However, they don't buy a book merely because the author has 4 million followers. This goes back to influence; your community forms around you because they feel they can benefit from what you have to offer and trust that you will provide valuable information. Your author's platform grows when people associate you and your name with something of benefit to them.

Earning a reputation as a trusted expert and inspiring word-of-mouth referrals (including "shares" or "likes") as an author and influencer is not as complicated as it seems. You need only do three things:

- **Be authentic.** Just be yourself. Let people know who you are and what you are about. Let them know what you care about most—your mission or cause. Do this with every status update you share and every blog post you publish.
- **Share your knowledge—freely.** Regularly provide great content related to the change you want to inspire and the transformation your target audience seeks. Do this with the station-satellite method, and your readers and followers will begin to trust you, like you, explore more of what you have to offer, and tell others about what they discover. They will also join your movement or take on the change you suggest. When your book is released, they will purchase it, too.
- **Show up consistently.** To make a difference online, you must participate in social media every week, if not every day. Have conversations or add to those already happening online in your subject area. Engage with your followers.

Employ the station and satellite method to attract your community and significantly increase your visibility and reach. As these elements grow, so do your authority and influence with your target market, which increases your potential to sell books and make a difference.

Many writers get overwhelmed with platform building—especially online. They feel they can't write and attract a community at the same time. You can hire someone to represent you and help with your networking, but your followers still expect to hear from you. Responding to comments or conversing with fans is not an activity you can delegate in its entirety. Nor can you hire someone to create or schedule all your status updates. Social media marketing doesn't work that way because it is interactive. Also, social media algorithms differentiate between auto-posted content and that which you manually upload. Therefore, you must be personally involved in your social networking efforts to some extent if you want to succeed as an Author of Change. This is especially true as you begin the journey to writing for change.

Even after reading this chapter, you might be thinking, "My time would be better spent writing a fabulous book." (More on that in Chapter 9 and 10.) Remember, creating change is the goal, and the book is a tool you use to achieve that result. If you are committed to your purpose and your book's purpose, your online efforts align perfectly with your mission. See online community building as just one more way to share your message and author change.

Rest assured, though, there are other ways to make a difference that do not involve the Internet. In the next chapter, you will learn how to expand and connect with your audience using both creative and traditional methods. These can also help your book change lives and the world.

8

MOTIVATE WITH CREATIVE AND TRADITIONAL TOOLS

"What counts in life is not the mere fact that we have lived. It is what difference we have made to the lives of others that will determine the significance of the life we lead."

— NELSON MANDELA

While the number of ways to reach a target market increases each year and book marketing approaches continually evolve, some strategies have survived the test of time. In addition to online efforts, an effective community building plan for an Author of Change includes both traditional and creative approaches. You may not feel able or willing to use all the tools available for sharing your message, but you can fill your toolbox with those that align with your values, skill set, and purpose to effectively attract your audience.

Now that you understand the online tools, let's explore more traditional ways of increasing your visibility, selling books, connecting with your audience, and making a positive and meaningful difference with your words.

Traditional Tools

Radio

Radio appearances can be fun, interesting, and effective. Making a guest appearances on a radio show is one of my favorite traditional mediums for sharing my message because it allows me to speak to thousands of people at one time from the comfort of my home—sometimes wearing my jammies. All that's required is a telephone line and the confidence to speak about your topic during a fifteen- to sixty-minute interview.

If your audience listens to any type of radio, including terrestrial and satellite radio as well as Internet radio or podcasts, create a media page on your website that makes available the essential materials needed by radio show hosts or managers. These include:

- A short bio—something that can be easily and quickly read as an introduction
- A professional headshot
- Two or three topics about which you can speak
- A list of questions the host can ask related to your book or the listed topics

While radio shows cover a plethora of subjects, find ones that specifically cover your book's subject area or that would be interested in your cause. Then, send each show's contact person an emailed pitch, which is like a query letter but shorter, with a compelling subject line. (See the Writing for Publication section below for more info on query letters.) The body of the email should quickly tell the show's director what you offer and why it is unique and interesting to the show's audience. Also provide a short bio that clarifies why you are the authority on the topic. Remember to include contact information and a link to your website media page.

Television

A television interview may seem like a pipe dream or something only for those with celebrity status, but it isn't. I know a woman who was writing a book to help women understand website creation. She made a connection with a local television show host, which turned into three appearances on the station's morning news show. Another colleague was asked to start a relationship advice column for a local newspaper. The column's success landed her a weekly television spot on the local station.

Research local television stations. Pitch them in the same way you pitch a radio station. However, keep in mind that television is a visual medium. The producer of any show will want to ensure you are an expert and that you sound and look like one as well. A photo helps convince them, but a video has more impact for this medium. Therefore, be sure your media page includes videos of you speaking. These can be clips of you presenting to a group, perhaps at a conference, or speaking directly to the camera, such as in a YouTube video.

Once you have one or two local television appearances under your belt, add these to your media page. Then, set your sights higher! Approach national television shows in the same manner.

Writing for Publications

I got my publishing start as a magazine journalist, and I still love this medium for aspiring authors because it involves writing. Plus, producing an article for a magazine or newspaper is not just a byline —a published credit—but a way to put your message in front of a new audience that likes to read and is interested in your cause. That means they also might purchase your book.

Pitching to a newspaper or magazine requires writing and sending a query letter to an editor. Follow these five steps to write a query letter, which you can also use when pitching radio or television stations:

- Include a compelling lead paragraph.
- Provide a brief outline of the scope of your article, who you will interview, and the length of the piece.
- Detail why this piece is perfect for this magazine.
- Offer a brief bio that illustrates why you are the right person to write this article.
- Provide links to your previously published work.

Research the publication before sending your query. Check the writers' bylines against the magazine's editorial staff to determine if the publication uses freelancers or staff writers. Carefully choose the right editor to whom to pitch your idea for an article.

Also, study the types and length of articles the magazine publishes, and pitch an idea that suits the publication's style, voice, and interests. You can pick from any number of article formats, including news, op-ed, lifestyle, personality profile, trend, or personal essay. One may lend itself better to your message than another or may best suit the publication's needs or requirements.

Send your query letter by email, unless the magazine's writers' guidelines indicate otherwise, and start your subject line with the word "query." Follow that with a compelling, succinct, subject statement.

Journalists often seek experts to interview for their articles. Join connectively.us,Presshunt.co, PRNewswire.com, and Pitchrate.com —or any other public relations services that allow journalists to seek experts and look at queries daily. By responding to relevant media requests, you may discover that it's easier to get quoted in articles than to write your own. Additionally, ExpertClick.com offers a chance to list yourself on the site as a subject-area expert so that you can be easily found by journalists, as well as send press releases that get seen by journalists. (Use my name for a discount!)

Public Speaking

Lots of writers prefer to remain the unseen face behind their work. However, you are more than just a writer. You are someone with a purpose to fulfill and a message to share. To do that effectively, share your spoken voice.

Public speaking is one of the most powerful change tools at your disposal. When someone can see and hear you speak in person, they connect with you personally. When your audience connects with you, you gain influence with them, which makes them more likely to buy into your message and movement.

You can develop a speech about your cause and seek out opportunities to speak to fifteen or twenty people at first, such as at a local MeetUp, your church, or a service organization. As your confidence builds, look for chances to speak to larger groups.

To land a speaking gig, you'll need:

- **A speaker's one-sheet**—This one-page document includes either a photo of you speaking or a headshot, a brief bio, a description of what you speak about, testimonials related to your speaking ability, and your contact information.
- **A speaking proposal**—Much like a query letter, this document explains what you'd like to speak about, why your topic is relevant to the audience, and why you are qualified to speak on that subject.

- **A payment structure**—If you want to get paid, the proposal you send also should state your speaking fees and travel expense compensation.
- **Proof of speaking ability**—In the proposal, include a list of previous speaking engagements, if you've done any. If you have not done public speaking to date, direct the event coordinator to your YouTube channel or a video of you speaking.

Be sure your website includes a speaker's page so those who visit know you are available to speak at their events.

Advertising

Paid advertising offers another way to get your message in front of more people and bring them into your community's fold. While advertising is not for everyone—and is often not within a writer's budget—it is a powerful tool, and you have more advertising options than ever before.

If you feel a bit queasy about advertising your book and cause, take to heart the words of Howard Gossage, an American advertising innovator, who said, "Advertising justifies its existence when used in the public interest—it is much too powerful a tool to use solely for commercial purposes."

There are a variety of types of advertising from which to choose. Let's look at a few.

- ### Direct Mail Campaigns

A classic advertising method involves sending information by mail to your target audience—yes, with a stamp from the post office. Obviously, you need to have a mailing list that includes physical addresses to use this strategy. If you do have such a list, consider the fact that direct mail campaigns get results. According to Small Business Trends, the average return on investment (ROI) for direct mail campaigns is between 18 and 20 percent. Fifty-six percent of consumers who responded to direct mail went online or visited the physical store. And a whopping 62 percent of consumers who responded to direct mail in the past three months made a purchase. Additionally, direct mail still pulls a higher response rate than any digital direct marketing medium —with response rates ranging from about five to nine times greater than those of email, paid search, or social media.

You can create your mailer—a brochure or postcard, for instance— using a service like Vista Print, which will even mail the document for you. Check out PSPrint.com and everydoordirectmail.com, companies that also provide distribution services.

- *Print Ads*

Placing an ad in a publication can grow your book sales and keep your movement growing. In the age of digital advertising, you might think print ads had lost their effectiveness; but the opposite is true. We tend to scroll by digital ads quickly, but print ads have credibility and grab attention. According to a BusinessTown.com article, "Consumers trust print ads in much larger numbers (71 percent) than they trust TV (41 percent) or online advertising (just 25 percent)." A Millward Brown study used fMRI scanning to observe how brain reactions differed when subjects were shown direct mail print ads versus the same ad on a screen and found that "tangible materials leave a deeper footprint on the brain." Our brains literally are built to better remember print than digital ads. Even millennials, who were born into the digital age, are more likely to pay attention to a print ad than one seen online.

The most effective advertising strategies will include a combination of digital and print ads. While social media advertising might reach more potential customers, print is more likely to reach your target audience.

- **Television Ads**

Think about how much money companies pay to run traditional ads on television during events like the Super Bowl—well over $5 million for 30 seconds of time in 2019. They spend big bucks because they can target a huge audience at one time, and television advertising continues to provide an enormously useful tool for sharing a message or selling a product.

Interestingly, according to an article by Brian Steinberg in *Variety*, Super Bowl advertising has trended toward cause-related advertising. "Since 2014, the experience of watching a Super Bowl has become akin to being immersed in a stream of consciousness conversation about profound changes in culture and socioeconomics. Recent Super Bowl ads have lectured viewers about diversity, gender pay equity, environmental sustainability, and immigration."

Television advertising can be costly; but if your cause has large financial supporters, consider using this tool to promote it.

- **Radio Ads**

Despite our digital age, people still listen to radio stations, and radio ads pack a lot of punch. According to a 2024 report on the consumer audio market by Deloitte, approximately 50 percent of people globally (4 billion) tune into radio. Eighty-two percent of US citizens listen to terrestrial radio every week, and 70 percent of the US population listens to online radio weekly. In Europe, 80 percent of adults listen to the radio daily, and 90 percent of the population listens weekly.

Your book represents your movement. Therefore, radio ads that direct people to purchase your book impact your movement's growth (and your book sales).

To get started, select stations that appeal to your target audience. Tailor your ads to the specific stations on which you advertise. Choose ad slots based on the times of day when your audience is listening to the radio. Radio advertisements are typically 30 seconds long, so your message needs to be clearly articulated and concise and must compel listeners to act. You can use your book pitch or your purpose statement in your radio ad, since they are short and easily understood.

Local stations might provide a more inexpensive route into radio advertising, but keep in mind that this marketing tool, while less expensive than television advertising, is still not cheap. Radio advertising can cost between $200 to $5,000 per week depending on location and the size of the listening audience. Run your ad more than once to increase the chances of brand recognition among the station listeners. Don't forget to consider the cost of radio ad production, which can range from $1,000 to $2,500 depending on what is included, like music, voice actors, and editing. Some stations have their own advertising production teams, and using them can save some expense.

- *Social Media Ads*

Social media ads offer a creative, nontraditional, and often less expensive way to advertise your book and cause. Today, advertising online is a well-accepted way to market just about anything—including a cause. If you want to mobilize a worldwide movement, do it on the World Wide Web. You can advertise on Google or Amazon as well as on some social networks, such as Facebook, Twitter, Pinterest, and Instagram.

Digital marketing—and specifically, social media advertising—has become a commonly used strategy because it helps you target people around the world who are most interested in your book or movement. Therefore, if you want a quick ROI for your ads, try social media advertising. Even if you don't get the desired results immediately, you will see an increase in referrals, followers, likes, and email subscribers, as well as in general reach, visibility, and authority in your target market. That, of course, leads to more influence and a larger community as well.

In many cases, people use social media specifically to make purchasing decisions. Consider that 97 percent of Gen Zers say social media is their top method for researching shopping options.

Social media has proven to be an effective way to bring attention to a cause. Imagine what putting a little advertising money behind yours might accomplish. Social media has helped such movements as #metoo, the It Gets Better Project, and the #BringBackOurGirls campaign, as well as popularizing the Human Rights Campaign's red equals sign—a successful example of visual branding for a movement. Your movement can reach a huge, targeted audience when you add a digital advertising campaign to your community building approach. To get the ROI you desire, advertise on sites used by your target audience and where these people actively engage with ads.

To create and manage your digital ad campaign, run them manually on your own, via automated software, or by hiring an advertising manager service to do it for you.

Before we move on, take a few moments to journal your answers to the following questions about traditional tools.

- Have you ever tried to get an article or op-ed published in a newspaper or magazine? Why or why not? If you succeeded, how can you replicate that success?
- Do you feel qualified to be interviewed by traditional media? What would make you feel qualified?
- Do you have the confidence necessary to appear on TV or radio? What would make you feel more confident?
- What do you have to offer journalists that would make them interested in covering you and your story, message, or cause?
- What special training have you had to prepare you to appear on radio or television? Do you feel you need training to do so? Where could you get such training?
- How can you improve your speaking skills?
- When, if ever, have you felt most comfortable talking to a live audience? What made you comfortable?
- Have you run an ad for something in the past? How did it perform?
- If you were to tackle advertising, what platforms or types of ads would make your book or movement most visible to your audience? Which one would be the easiest for you to learn, manage, and afford?
- What is the one thing that currently stops you from utilizing traditional tools to promote or market your book and cause? How can you overcome that obstacle?

Creative and Nontraditional Tools

Let's explore some creative and nontraditional tools you can use to increase your audience size, sell books, and become more visible to those interested in your cause.

Email Lists and Campaigns

In today's world, email marketing—sending commercial messages to a group of people via email—offers an enormously effective way to market anything. It is also your most powerful platform element.

Those who opt into your mailing list have indicated their desire for you to keep them apprised about your cause, products, services, and book. By opting in to receive emails from you on a regular basis, people give you permission to contact and sell to them.

Additionally, you have a unique opportunity to create a personal relationship with email subscribers. You can not only tell your subscribers about your book's release, speaking events, or new developments related to your movement but also share with them your thoughts, challenges, and accomplishments. You can even ask them to answer questions or reply to your emails.

Despite the fact that email open and click-through rates have dropped significantly, email marketing is still effective; it's just a bit harder to get the attention of your subscribers. Campaign Monitor's research on Email Marketing Benchmarks for 2020 pointed out that industries like media, entertainment, publishing, and nonprofits enjoy some of the highest click-through rates—3.02 percent on average. That's good news for an Author of Change; it means more people in these industries get subscribers to click on links.

Effective email marketing depends on your ability to write emails and headlines that engage your audience. But email marketing is inexpensive and can be done by anyone. You will need to use an email marketing system, like Infusionsoft, Mail Chimp, Aweber, or Active Campaign. With that in place, you can ask people to join your list and nurture those relationships with regular email messages. Keep in mind that you need to give people a reason to join your mailing list. Usually, this is accomplished with a free-but-valuable piece of content called a lead magnet. It can be a simple PDF providing tips or steps toward desired change.

Today, most online marketers—including authors—include an email launch in their marketing plans. Your book will be sold online; thus, your marketing plan should include an email campaign as well, which can include a *buy link* in each email sent. So, start thinking about how to grow an email list as soon as possible, such as by having followers on social media opt into your lead magnet or join your list via teleseminar, webinar, or some other type of live virtual event.

Teleseminars

Content marketing involves the creation and sharing of valuable material online, such as videos and free courses as well as books, blog posts, or social media updates. These materials do not explicitly promote a brand but are intended to stimulate interest in products or services. As you build out your content marketing plan, consider using teleseminars to share your message. Teleseminars are meetings held by phone using a teleconferencing service, like Freeconfer encecall.com. A teleseminar involves inviting people—via social media and email—to attend an event or meeting where you share information about your movement or book. Attendees listen to your presentation either on the telephone or with a computer or other device connected to the internet.

You need a registration page (usually located on your website) that allows you to capture registrants' name and email address so you can send them the call-in information, reminders, and any follow-up information. (Teleseminar registrants end up on your email list, which makes this a great list-building strategy.)

Teleseminars are most often used as an online educational tool. Research suggests that the online education industry will exceed

$325 billion by 2025. See teleseminars as a way to educate your audience about your cause and to inspire members to act now to create change. Additionally, those who attend your teleseminars are likely to purchase your book.

Teleseminars are easy to manage and inexpensive—even free—to host. If you are an introvert or afraid of being seen on video or in person, a phone call with some people interested in your movement should feel doable. After all, it's just a conversation. Just share about the change you want to create with the excitement and commitment you have for it.

Webinars

Much like teleseminars, webinars offer a way to share your message, teach, and gather engaged community members as you provide valuable content, using video as well as audio in this case. Inside Sales reported that 73 percent of sales and marketing leaders listed webinars as one of the best ways to generate top-quality leads for businesses. (As an author, you are in the publishing business.) Many people register for and attend one webinar per week for up to an hour, and 92 percent of GoToWebinar.com users agree that webinars are the best way to engage a large, remote audience, such as those who will read your book. Like teleseminars, webinars are a powerful email list building tool.

Webinars are not hard to run. Invite people to your event using email and social media. You typically need to set up a registration page on your website. Host the webinar using an online videoconferencing service like Zoom.com, Webinarjam.com, or Gotowebinar.com. However, there are free services as well, such as what is offered by Freeconferencecall.com. Additionally, some webinar services allow you to stream directly to Facebook, LinkedIn, and YouTube.

During a webinar, those who attend see you speaking on video. You can connect with your audience in a much more powerful way then with written or audio content, including answering your attendees' questions and engaging with them live. Again, this increases that know-like-trust factor, which increases your influence.

Online Groups

In the "old days" of the Internet, the only way to gather people around your cause online was with a forum built into your website. Today, forums have been replaced with online groups created on social media sites like Facebook and LinkedIn, or hosted by services like MightyNetworks.com or Discord.com.

An online group or community consists of site users with similar interests who gather to explore and converse about a topic. You can set the privacy of these groups, making them quite intimate if you like. Most authors, change makers, entrepreneurs, and online marketers use social media groups and pages to build and engage with their target audiences.

You can create groups on LinkedIn and Facebook, for example. Facebook has at least 150 groups with over a million followers. Imagine starting one related to your book and cause and growing it to even a fraction of that size. You might find yourself with a lot of influence and impact in your target market, making it much easier to inspire change with or without a book.

There's not much to using this creative tool. If you have an account on a social media site that offers groups, create one using an intuitive process. Or choose a different tool for your virtual group.

Your Own Radio Show

Consider starting your own radio show. Many companies like Voice America and Blog Talk Radio will happily host your show, but sometimes a fee is involved.

On the other hand, you could start a podcast. Podcasts have become extremely popular, and you don't need to spend a lot of money to launch one. You do need a page on your website to host the audio files. The show needs a name with corresponding artwork, and each episode requires a short write-up, called "show notes," to explain what the show is about. Plus, you will need a delivery system (like iTunes), as well as a hosting company such as Blubrry or Lybsyn. Additionally, recording equipment, including a microphone, a headset, and an audio recording and editing program, is required. Alternatively, you can hire someone to help with editing.

A YouTube TV Station

Create a YouTube station if you want a creative and nontraditional approach to television. Many people today use YouTube channels as their television stations, even featuring live appearances. YouTube is second only to Facebook in its number of users and is a powerful search engine that pulls up videos in response to keyword searches. If you optimize your YouTube videos well—choosing relevant keywords and strong descriptions that make your videos easily discoverable in an online search—you may find this medium a fantastic way to become a TV host in your own right and to create an engaged community of people interested in the transformation you offer.

Keep this important fact in mind: People who watch a video retain 95 percent of a message, compared to 10 percent of what they read in text. Plus, videos generate a higher conversion rate, which means people more often tend to make purchases after watching a video.

You will be selling a book and may already be promoting a cause. Online shoppers find video helps their decision-making process. Video can sell viewers on your brand of change, get them to buy into your movement, and encourage them to purchase your book. In fact, including video on a sales page can increase conversion by 80 percent, and 64 percent of those who watch a sales video are likely to purchase.

If you wonder if anyone will watch your video, consider that according to Hyperfine Media, one-third of online activity is time spent watching videos. People watch videos because they are fun, interesting, and easy to consume, but they also increase your audience's ability to know you. That leads to the coveted know-like-trust factor that increases book sales.

Blogging and Emailed Newsletters

Blogging and newsletters provide creative ways to approach article publication. I mentioned blogging previously as a great way to increase your visibility online and become an expert.

Newsletters also help attract an audience, especially with the availability of Substack.com, which allows you to publish your newsletter to its audience and even build an email list there. You can create a newsletter on the topic of your book or on subjects related to your cause and send it to email subscribers and promote it on social media as well.

Both blogging and newsletters provide the freedom to write what you choose and share your content, which draws people to subscribe to your mailing list.

Virtual Speaking Gigs

As a guest featured on a virtual event, you can be involved in public speaking as part of an online summit, by hosting a masterclass, or as a participant in any video streaming to YouTube or Facebook.

You can host your own online speaking event, which is a creative and nontraditional way to use this tool. For instance, create your own summit and invite five or more experts to speak over the course of a day or an entire week; your expert status, audience, and influence will increase as a result. Like a webinar or teleseminar, you need to promote the event and provide a way for people to register so you can send connection information. Registrants are placed on a mailing list, which makes these types of virtual events superb email list building tools. Plus, your guests will promote the event, putting you and your cause in front of their audience, effectively increasing your own.

Online summits in your subject area are a powerful and easy way to reach a global audience. Pitch the organizers of such events as you would make a pitch to radio or television shows. Such virtual events often have planners who scan the Internet looking for appropriate experts. If you have done the work to make yourself, your book, and your cause visible online, they will find you with a simple Google search, and you won't have to pitch them at all.

To determine which of these creative and nontraditional tools are suited to you, your book, and your cause, take a moment to answer the following questions in your journal.

1. Do you have an email list? How could you encourage your target audience to subscribe to your list?

2. How could you use a teleseminar or a series of webinars to promote your cause and book and build your email list?

3. Are you comfortable enough speaking virtually? What would help you feel more comfortable?

4. Do you feel ready and able to create and run virtual events of your own? What skills do you need to learn to utilize this tool?

5. Do you have a social media account that allows you to form a group related to your book? If so, have you created a group? If not, what type of group could you start right away to attract people to your cause? If you don't want to do this on social media, what tool do you choose to use to create an online community?

6. Have you thought about hosting your own radio or television show? What would it take for you to feel ready to do so?

7. Of all the creative tools mentioned in this chapter, which ones best suit you, your cause, and your comfort level? Which one would be the most powerful in terms of building an audience but might require you to stretch to use it?

8. Are you more comfortable with traditional or creative methods of building community? Regardless of your answer, which type of community building tool would be most effective for you and your cause?

With the variety of traditional and creative marketing tools at your disposal, you can find at least a few ways to create an engaged community around your cause. Use them consistently and you'll increase your influence and visibility with your target audience. You'll also grow your audience. Then, you can turn your attention to writing your book and authoring change in the world knowing you have a community ready and eager to purchase your book and implement your change strategies.

PART THREE
HOW TO AUTHOR CHANGE

9

PREPARE TO WRITE A TRANSFORMATIONAL BOOK

"The people who are crazy enough to think they can change the world are the ones who do."

— STEVE JOBS

I f you've completed the exercises in this book, you should have a clear idea of the book you want to write. However, it behooves you to take time to make sure that your idea supports writing the best book possible—one with the highest likelihood of selling, getting read, and making a positive and meaningful difference. Accomplishing that goal takes a bit of writing prep work. It's time to develop a writing plan to help you fulfill your book's purpose as you write with ease and focus.

To author the change you want to see in the world, you can write a novel, memoir, parable, biography, or prescriptive nonfiction book. Historically, though, nonfiction has offered a powerful vehicle for change. With that in mind, consider the types of books that have motivated you to change, started movements in the past, or reached millions of readers around the globe. And while you may be experienced in one genre, like fiction, and feel inclined to write a change-inspiring novel, now is the time to consider stretching your writing skills, possibly by switching genres so that your message will have the most impact.

Books about change can not only span multiple genres but various topics and niches as well. You can write a book meant to help readers achieve personal transformation. For instance, your book could focus on individual change, such as how to be an effective leader, lose weight, access spiritual guidance, or overcome grief. If you intend to spark organizational, social, or global change, your book might focus on motivating innovation, celebrating diversity, or stopping global warming. The subjects you can tackle are as numerous as the problems, causes, or issues facing humanity at any given time.

Consider how writing a book is like planting a tree. It begins with a seed—an idea. Out of this seed sprout roots—your book's purpose—that grow deep into the ground. The trunk begins as a tiny sapling that breaks through the earth and grows tall and strong—the book's table of contents. The trunk sprouts branches—the topics you will cover in each chapter—as well as twigs and leaves—additional points you will make about each topic. By the time you finish writing, you have created a full-grown tree—a book watered with your purpose and fertilized by readers who sit in its shade and consume its fruits: inspiration, motivation, answers, solutions, and new strategies for thinking and behaving.

Trees take a long time to become big enough to create shade or bear fruit. The same could be said of writing a book. You can speed up your writing process with a writing guide consisting of a *table of contents* and *chapter summaries* or *outlines*. Add to these your purpose and your book's purpose, and you have a clear roadmap to get from planting to harvest. Your writing guide breaks down the steps necessary to complete a manuscript, thus making writing a long-form book feel doable and enjoyable. Plus, it allows you to write more effectively.

Before we create your writing guide, though, you must complete a preliminary step: Identify your ideal reader.

Your Ideal Reader

When you write a book, it's imperative to know who will read it. Only with a clear picture of your ideal reader can you produce a book that targets that person's needs. In Chapter 2, you identified your audience, which is also your book's market or ideal reader. In Chapter 6, I suggested speaking to your ideal reader as you engage in community building activities. You created a customer avatar—a profile or description of this person. That avatar represents the person for whom you are writing.

Expand the information on your ideal reader into a market or audience analysis, which includes any adjacent or additional audiences that might purchase your book as well as the size of these markets. Arming yourself with details about your market size gets you thinking about whether your book's content would be more effective if directed toward a larger or smaller audience or additional markets.

Complete a market analysis by conducting online research to discover statistics that describe the size of your book's target audience. Don't describe your market as "people like me who stand up for women's rights," for example. Instead, describe the market as "the half million people—primarily women—who participated in the first Women's March on January 21, 2017" or "the estimated 4 million Women's March participants across the US and the hundreds of sister marches in other US cities and abroad plus all those who participated in the Women's March in subsequent years." Notice how specific this is about who makes up your market and how many of those people exist in the world. The more specific you can be about your market, the easier it becomes to write your book.

In the process of this analysis, you might realize you need to change your audience. If your market is too big and unspecified, focus in on your core constituency. Instead of your book being for all women (more than 4 billion globally or over 49 percent of the world population, according to Countrymeters.info), your market might be directed at the four million people—mostly women—who participated in the first Women's March in 2017. What can you find out about female activists? For instance, do most of them have children? If so, maybe your audience is specifically mothers interested in women's rights. Or if you want to impact women business owners, your book might be better directed at the more than 13.8 million firms owned by women in the U.S.—or the 28.6 percent of women who own businesses with a revenue of $1 million or more. Consider whether your book will be more successful if it is tailored for a more specific niche or even for additional markets. (Yes, you can have more than one market, but you still want to write for *a reader*—your customer avatar—who is a composite of those audiences.)

When you've completed your market analysis, write a short description of your market, or perhaps of each audience segment you intend to target with your book, community building actions, and marketing plans. The more specifically you identify your markets, the better chance you have of writing a book that motivates the members of that audience to change. Then, revisit the reader profile you created previously and see if it needs to be altered.

Write for a specific reader. As you write, converse with this reader through your written words.

Hone Your Idea with Models and Competition

Developing an outline or table of contents for your book represents an essential step in creating your writing guide. I don't recommend finalizing your book's structure or beginning to write until you've completed a two-part analysis meant to help you develop a sound and unique book structure. First, analyze books you've found inspirational, motivational, and transformational. Second, analyze your book's direct competition, which consists of other books published on the topic. These analyses inform the structure and content of your book, and once complete, they support you in creating a table of contents or outline for your book, allowing you to compose chapter summaries or a more detailed outline. Then, you are ready to begin writing and the writing will flow logically from chapter to chapter and topic to topic.

Other transformational books can influence how you structure and write your own. As Tony Robbins says, "Success leaves clues," and these change-inspiring books are filled with clues about how they succeeded. Emulating these models can aid in your efforts to develop an appropriate and effective book structure and write your manuscript with confidence.

To begin your two-part analysis, answer the following six questions in your journal:

- What three books have inspired you to change?
- What made these books' messages motivational?
- What type of "voice" did the authors use—authoritative, scholarly, conversational, formal, friendly, or something else?
- What three things about each of these books motivated you to action?
- How did the authors or books make you feel, and how did they accomplish that?

- Why did these books make such a big impression on you?

Consider how you can replicate the inspirational and motivational aspects of these books. To discern how an author made you want to change, review Chapter 3; determine if the author used any of the change mechanisms discussed. For instance, if your favorite transformational book included a story at the beginning of each chapter and you connected deeply with the author through those stories, you may want to include a story at the beginning of your chapters, too. Brendon Burchard does this in *High Performance Habits*, as does Gabby Bernstein in *The Universe Has Your Back*. Or if the author included a set of action items at the end of each chapter and you enjoyed doing those exercises, maybe you want to do the same. Bo Eason did this in his book *There's No Plan B for Your A Game*, as did Darren Hardy in *The Compound Effect*.

Common Elements in Books Make a Difference

Next, review your book's direct competition to determine which potential rival books provide the best models. Examine your book's idea, structure, and content with an eye toward making it unique and necessary in the category where it will be sold, such as self-help, business, body/mind/spirit, or environmental science. Study books with concepts similar to your idea that are bestsellers in the primary category in which your book will be sold. These books should be recent—published in the last five years or due to be released in the next twelve months. Do this research on Amazon.com and barne sandnoble.com as well as in a physical bookstore. Find five titles that are closest in subject matter to your book idea which you believe are direct competition—these are titles you believe someone might buy instead of your book or vice versa. Look carefully at each book's table of contents, introduction, foreword, back cover copy, special features, and the author's bio. Read a bit or all of each book. Check out the books' reviews to find clues about how they could have been improved or what the author did well. Make notes of what you think is positive or negative about each book.

In your journal, answer these questions about the books you've identified as competition:

1. How could you incorporate the elements or characteristics you love about these books into your project?
2. Of the change-inspiring elements in the books, which ones could you include in a similar fashion in your book?
3. How is each book structured, and could that structure work for your book?
4. Did the author include any special features, such as exercises, a workbook section, success stories, or action items? Would adding similar elements help the structure and content of your book?
5. How long was each book, and is that an appropriate length for your book? Did you wish the book was longer or shorter?
6. How long were the book's chapters? Did you wish they were longer or shorter, and what length would be best for your chapters?
7. Is there anything else about these books that you feel made them successful that you could use as a role model for yours?

You can also create a chart like the one below in your journal. Then use it to compare and contrast the top five bestselling competitive books. Identify the pros, cons, and noteworthy aspects of these books.

Book Title	Pro	Con	Noteworthy

Conducting a competitive analysis helps you brainstorm ways to improve your idea and make it stand out from other titles on the bookstore shelf. In your journal, answer this question: Knowing my competition, how can I make my book more marketable?

Then, brainstorm all the ways you could improve your book project. Might you include some sort of workbook element or another special feature? Do you need to interview experts? Could you incorporate anything you noticed in the competitive titles you analyzed?

Consider incorporating into your book project what other authors did well, eliminating or avoiding what they did poorly, and finding ways to include whatever you found missing or noteworthy in these other books into your book. (Obviously, I am not suggesting plagiarizing content.)

Create a Table of Contents

Now, it's time to create your table of contents. This is the fun part—designing the "trunk" or structure of your book.

If you have no idea how to create a table of contents, try these three methods.

1. *Teach*: What process would you use to teach someone how to create the change you propose? How would you describe that change and why they would want to create such transformation? That's your first chapter. Then, what steps do they need to take to reach transformation? Each step provides the basis for a chapter. You might also devise a final chapter that wraps up any loose ends or tells them what to do next.

2. *Create an outline*: Most of us have created a project outline before. As you brainstorm book content, jot down your ideas and organize them into first-level, second-level, and third-level line items. First-level items become chapters, which become part of the table of contents. Second-level line items typically make great subheadings followed by appropriate content. Third-level line items might be sub-subheadings followed by related content.

3. *Create a mind map*: If you are visually inclined or often find yourself overthinking, a mind map helps get your ideas onto paper. Then, you can organize them into a book structure. A mind map is an effective way to brainstorm without worrying about order and structure initially, returning to organize your ideas later. When you mind map the structure of a book, you diagram your content ideas, link related ones, and arrange them all around a central concept—the topic of your book. This type of non-linear graphical layout builds an intuitive framework around a central concept. You can create a mind map on a piece of paper, a white board, or using a mind mapping app or program. (I go into more detail about how to do this below; also, see Chapter 7 for mind mapping examples.)

For nonfiction, create ten to twenty topics that reflect a logical progression or explanation of your subject. Most nonfiction trade books (those not written for academic or specialty markets) contain approximately this number of chapters, although the specific number depends on the complexity of the topic. Further refine these topics into subtopics that become the building blocks of a chapter.

For fiction, create characters that have their own backstories and motivations so you get to know them before setting them within the dramatic or comedic arc of your creation. Then create a storyline that includes the scenes, themes, and dramatic arcs. This becomes your outline. A memoir is mapped out in a similar fashion to a work of fiction, except your characters are not fictional. Although the story-line is your own, it still needs a story arc and character trans-formation.

A literary agent or acquisitions editor—as well as a potential reader —will read your table of contents with an eye toward understanding what your book is about. There is plenty of room for creativity, but if your book does not have a strong structure, the message can get lost, and then you won't impact readers; in fact, you'll lose the chance to influence anyone as soon as they look at a weak table of contents.

Mind Mapping Your Table of Contents

Mind mapping, a visual brainstorming tool, provides a creative exer-cise for developing a book's table of contents or outline. It's also a good way to determine your memoir's or novel's storyline and scenes. As mentioned in Chapter 7, you can purchase mind mapping software, such as MindNode or MindJet, or you can download free software like Freemind. The easiest way to complete this exercise, though, involves purchasing a large poster board and some colored pens or Post-it notes. You can use a large white board with erasable markers as well.

I recommend using a poster board and Post-it notes if you don't want to create your mind map on the computer. Place a large Post-it note in the middle of the board, and write your topic, book title, or message on it. Then brainstorm potential content. Write main topics on large sticky notes and related topics or stories on smaller or differently colored ones. Stick the notes all over the board. Don't worry about where you put them unless you know they are related subjects, in which case group them together.

When you run out of topics or stories, begin organizing the notes on the board into related subject areas. Pick up the sticky notes and move them around. The largest groupings become chapters. Use a different colored Post-it note at the top of each grouping to indicate the chapter name or topic. If you get additional ideas during this process, add them to the appropriate chapter grouping.

When finished, type each chapter name or subject into a document based on the most logical sequence. This becomes your book's table of contents.

To mind map a novel or memoir, use the same basic process, but place all the events on sticky notes. Then, organize them into a story-line. Put all your ideas for the story on various notes and move them around, combine them into scenes, and organize the scenes into chapters.

Using a computer program, your mind map might start out looking like this:

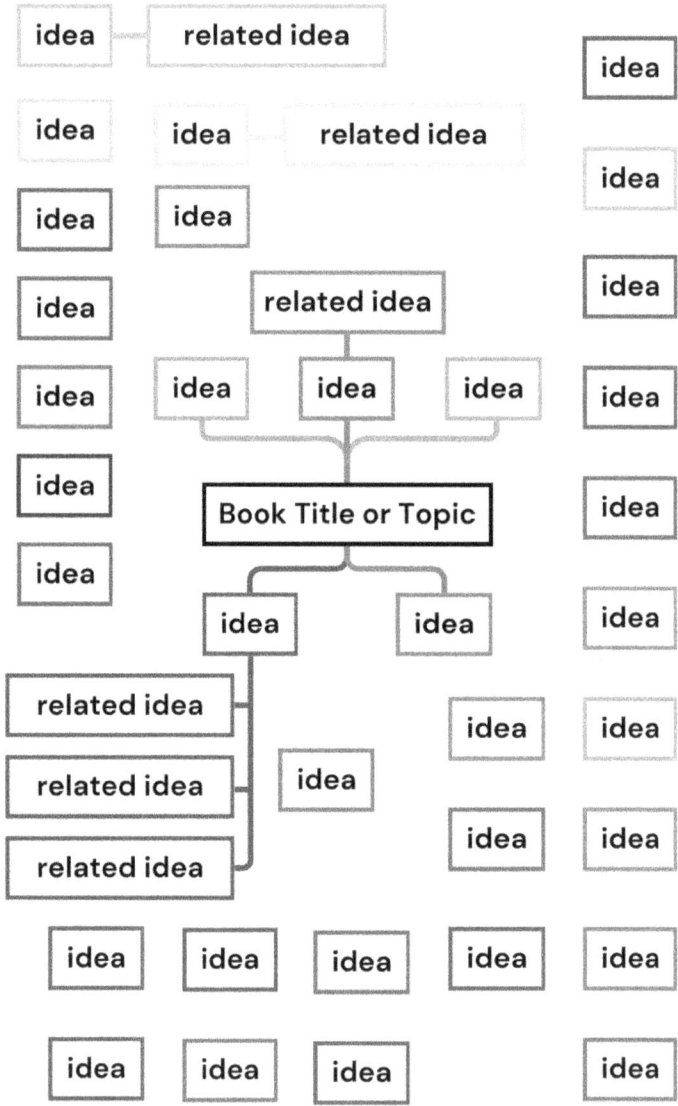

After you organize all your ideas, a book structure will emerge. Your mind map then looks like this—with defined chapters and ideas of what content to include in each of them.

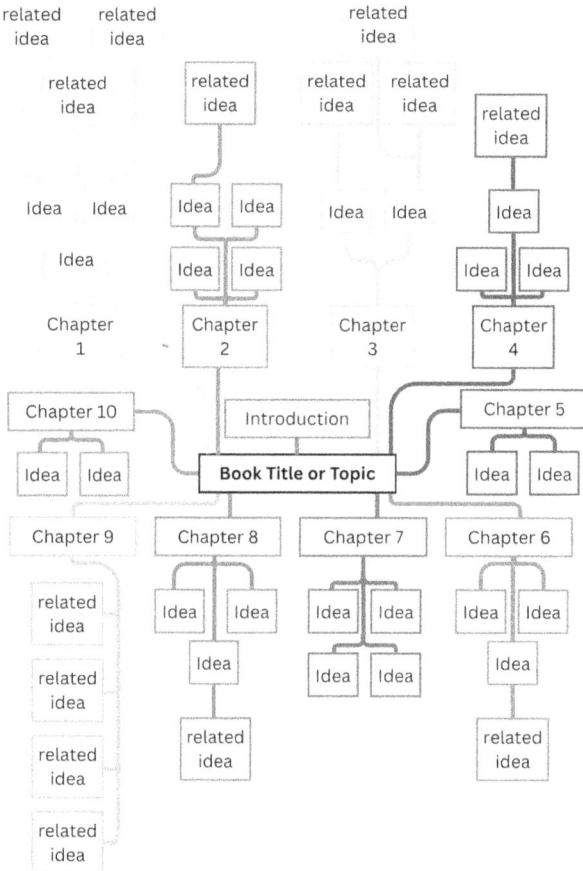

Give each chapter a title, and there you have a table of contents.

If you are struggling to create your table of contents, here are a few suggestions.

- Develop a list of ten to fifteen topics you know you want to cover and sequence them in the order you want to cover them.
- Think of ten to fifteen questions you want to answer for your readers and the order in which you want to answer each one.
- Look at the list of benefits your book will provide readers. Expand on this list if necessary so you have ten to fifteen benefits, each of which you can then address in a chapter.
- If you are writing a novel or memoir, create a storyboard that indicates where chapters start and finish.

Evaluate Your Book's Table of Contents

After you've created the first draft of your table of contents, look at it as one unit so you can see your book's big picture. Then answer these questions in your journal:

1. Does the book structure make logical sense?
2. Does your table of contents have an order that reflects a beginning, middle, and end?
3. Is the story, benefit, or message apparent?
4. Is it obvious why your audience would want to purchase this book?
5. Does the table of contents clearly demonstrate the journey the book takes readers on or how it gets them from where they are to where they want to go?

A potential reader—as well as a literary agent or acquisitions editor —will read your table of contents with an eye toward understanding your book. You have plenty of room for creativity, but your book's table of contents must have a logical structure that clearly demonstrates what the book is about and the benefit it offers. If it doesn't, you'll lose the chance to influence anyone—agent, editor, or reader —as soon as they look at the table of contents. Publishing professionals also look at the table of contents to determine marketability —if the book is unique enough to sell. If they don't believe readers will buy the published book, they won't purchase the manuscript from you.

Approaching book concept development with an eye to sales may seem unspiritual or inauthentic. You may want to dive into writing, allowing your intuition and creativity to guide you, and just hope for the best. But without a writing "map," you may meander off course, and the detour might cost you ten hours of writing and ten thousand unusable words (or more). You might write in a roundabout manner that produces a manuscript with so many twists and turns readers can't understand your message, which could cost fifty or more hours of editing and revising. Avoid these scenarios by ensuring you have a complete writing map before you begin and being willing to wear both creative and marketing hats at the same time. By combining your intuition with your reasoning abilities, you stand a better chance of fulfilling your purpose than by relying on inspiration alone. Take a business-like approach to your content, and you will write a book that targets your market, provides benefits readers desire, is unique and necessary in its category, and has the potential to change lives—or the world.

After completing a first draft and evaluating what you have created, review your table of contents one more time with an eye toward making it search-engine friendly. Fine-tune each chapter title so it includes a keyword. According to Moz.com, "Keywords are ideas and topics that define what your content is about. In terms of SEO, they're the words and phrases that searchers enter into search engines, also called 'search queries.' If you boil everything on your page—all the images, video, copy, etc.—down to simple words and phrases, those are your primary keywords." You want your book to be easily found in a Google or Amazon search for its subject. Therefore, its title, description, and chapter titles should contain keywords.

You know what your audience wants and needs and what information your book will provide. Use that knowledge to make a list of the keywords and keyword phrases someone might put into a search engine. They might be asking Google "how to lead consciously," "steps to becoming a foster parent," "how to open my third eye," "how to get over heartbreak," or the "best way to reduce greenhouse gases." Knowing the types of online searches your potential readers might conduct gives you the ability to include some of those terms in your book's title, subtitle, and chapter titles. You can also include these words in the back-cover description of your book. This process helps your book becomes discoverable online.

If you don't know what type of searches your audience is making, remember their pain points—the stresses they want to ease. Also refresh your memory about their problems and struggles. They are searching online for solutions, answers, and strategies. Do a bit of keyword research: For example, if you are writing a book about women's rights, go to Google Trends or sign up for a Google ad account and use the site's keyword planner to see what people are researching in that subject area. When you input a word or phrase into these tools, they display similar phrases or words people have entered into search engines. (You do not need to pay for advertising to use the Google keyword tool.) Additionally, you can use other free keyword tools, like Soovle on SEO.com or Ubersuggest on neilpatel.com. Many paid keyword tools exist as well.

Develop Chapter Outlines

Once you have completed your table of contents—the trunk of the tree—it's time to develop the branches and leaves. The primary branches, which sprout directly from the trunk, are the chapters themselves. Many twigs grow from the boughs—the subtopics or ideas you brainstormed when creating your mind map or outline. In a nonfiction book, the twigs equate to chapter subheadings; in a novel or memoir, they are scenes. Each chapter includes many small subjects—the leaves. In nonfiction, these might be a variety of points or stories covered in each subheading's section. For fiction or memoir, these could be the details—small incidents, descriptions, and characters—that make up a scene, tie the scenes together, or provide additional information.

Creation of the next part of your writing guide—a detailed chapter-by-chapter outline—involves planning chapter content. This outline will become your comprehensive writing map. By writing from point to point, your manuscript stays on track and you avoid detours. That means you get from start to finish easily and effectively and write the book you intend to write.

Go back to your mind map and flesh out the content in each chapter—the twigs and leaves. Each important topic within the chapter structure now becomes a subheading or scene to write. The additional Post-it notes indicate information you'll cover in the subheading area or scene.

Type the information into an outline. The document should look like a detailed table of contents or even an organized list of bullet points. You can use the template below to make this task easier.

Nonfiction Book Title or Topic

- **Introduction**
- **Chapter 1 - Title**
  - *Subheading – topic*
    - Point 1
    - Point 2
    - Point 3
    - Point 4
  - *Subheading – topic*
    - Point 1
    - Point 2
    - Point 3
    - Point 4
  - *Subheading – topic*
    - Point 1
    - Point 2
    - Point 3
    - Point 4
  - *Subheading – topic*
    - Point 1
    - Point 2
    - Point 3
    - Point 4

For fiction or memoir, you would include scenes and details about those scenes.

Fiction or Memoir Book Title

- **Chapter 1 - Title**
  - *Scene*
    - Details
    - Details
    - Details
    - Details
  - *Scene*
    - Details
    - Details
    - Details
    - Details
  - *Scene*
    - Details
    - Details
    - Details
    - Details
  - *Scene*
    - Details
    - Details
    - Details
    - Details

No matter how you decide to publish your book, your detailed outline or bullet list serves as your writing guide. You might want to go one step further, though, and include a few sentences for each item to help you understand and remember later what you intended to write. If you plan to publish traditionally, eventually you will craft your outline into chapter summaries or a synopsis that consists of a few paragraphs. A nonfiction book proposal requires chapter summaries that include strong prose describing each chapter and demonstrating your voice and writing ability.

As you finish up your book's detailed outline, take a moment to consider the length of each chapter. After all, you don't want to write a book that is too long—or too short. The average nonfiction book contains about 50,000 words; the average novel or memoir runs about 90,000 words. You may not know the final word count for each of your chapters at this point, but you can look at the planned content and estimate the length of each chapter. You might even write one chapter or several sections of a chapter and use that sample to calculate the average estimated length per chapter.

Additionally, look at the chapter length of your book models. Do you want your chapters approximately the same length as in your exemplars, or would you prefer to keep yours shorter or longer? Estimate the word count of each chapter by averaging the number of words per line and multiplying that amount by the average number of lines per page. Then multiply your calculation by the number of pages in an average chapter to arrive at the average length of that specific book's chapters. Use that calculation as a marker for your own chapters.

Once you know the approximate word count for each of your book's chapters, determine the word count for the entire manuscript. Multiply the average word count per chapter by the number of chapters in your table of contents. It's important to know the total word count so you can ensure your manuscript ends up within the average length of similar books. Publishers require an estimated word count to determine potential printing costs, and if you self-publish, the same holds true.

Also, you don't want to write more than necessary. While some writers struggle to write enough to meet a required word count, others tend to compose more words than are required. In either case, try to write only the number of words you need to avoid the painful and time-consuming process of cutting your manuscript down to size.

Prepare to Write

You are now ready to write. You have your writing guide—your book's table of contents and detailed chapter outlines. Plus, your mission keeps you focused on the result you want to achieve, and your book's purpose provides a GPS as you write. All that's left is for you to craft a manuscript that inspires and motives readers to change. Before putting your hands on the keyboard, it's worthwhile to consider how best to write a book that truly makes a difference. Sure, you can write your book as you would write any other book—or you can employ tools and tactics that have helped other authors compose books that impacted millions of lives.

Begin by bolstering your writing-for-change skills. Successful change agents know how to get people to do things differently. They may have studied the art of influence and persuasion or mastered personal growth techniques, sales tactics, or habit formation strategies. I've included essential information on how to inspire and motivate change in Chapter 3. Review that chapter before beginning and keep those strategies top of mind as you write.

If you need to know more about how human beings change, you can find a plethora of books and courses on the topic. For instance, you might read *Change: How to Make Things Happen* by Damon Centola, *Influence: The Psychology of Persuasion* by Robert Cialdini, or *Switch: How to Change Things When Change is Hard* by Dan and Chip Heath. Or take a course on neuro-linguistic programing (NLP) or persuasion. Such knowledge will enhance your ability to write a manuscript that moves readers to new action.

Studying successful transformational books helps you discover what worked well for other authors. Your previous research on models and competition offers a great starting place to analyze how successful change agents wrote their books. Go back to that list and look for similarities in how the books were written; consider how to implement what you learn. For instance, many change-inspiring books include research or data, while others utilize stories or personal anecdotes. Also, most change-inspiring books are written in a manner or voice that makes them:

- inviting
- personal
- relatable
- passionate
- authoritative
- aspirational

Additionally, transformational books:

1. **Contain the author's message or story**—Stories are relatable. As such, they are effective mechanisms for connecting with readers and helping them understand a message. Memoirs, like *Educated*, naturally do a good job of this. It's easy to forget about stories when writing prescriptive nonfiction, but you'll want to use stories to illustrate your message. *Talking to Strangers* (or any of Gladwell's books) does this well.

2. **Showcase the author's authentic voice**—Write from your heart and talk to—not at—your readers. As a result, readers quickly know, like, and trust you, which is the trifecta of influence. Think about the authors whose voices you love and whose books sound precisely as they speak, and follow their lead. Good examples are Kamal Ravikant's *Love Yourself Like Your Life Depends on It*, Cheryl Strayed's *Wild*, and Gabrielle Bernstein's *The Universe has Your Back*.

3. **Offer hope**—Change-inspiring books are hopeful, encouraging, and shed light. Readers need to feel as if there is a chance for transformation or they are unlikely to change. *No One Is Too Small to Make a Difference* and *Educated* fall into this category.

4. **Fill a need in the market**—Your book must be marketable. It must sell and be read to create change. Develop a book idea that features a unique angle on the subject matter and fills a gap on bookstore shelves. Answer frequently asked questions, provide solutions to common problems, address an unmet need in the marketplace, or choose a topic often queried in search engines. *This Changes Everything* combines environmental concerns with issues related to capitalism, giving it a unique angle on often-searched topics. That said, almost any book found on the *New York Times* nonfiction bestseller list fills a market need; that's why it sold enough copies to make it onto the list.

5. **Add value**— A book's benefits equate to its value. Readers don't care what your book is about as much as how reading it will benefit them, their organization, or the world. Most books list their benefits or provide a description or synopsis on the back cover that makes them apparent. For instance, the back-cover description of *This Changes Everything* says, "...we can seize this existential crisis to transform our economic system and build something radically better."

6. **Rely on well-researched data and persuasive arguments**—Nonfiction books about change often provide research, studies, data, anecdotes, success stories, or statistics to prove the validity of the author's arguments. While it poses a challenge, it's also possible to creatively work concrete data into a memoir. For instance, you can relate how you first read about a study online or discovered research in a newspaper article. Persuasion relies on convincing arguments. You must convince your readers there is good reason to change; otherwise, you'll struggle to get them on board. Read any one of the

aforementioned books, and you will find concrete data backing up arguments—even if that data was collected from personal experience.

7. **Feature the author's expert status, authority, or experience—** If you write nonfiction, your expertise, authority, and experience inform your book's premise and content. If you write a memoir, these come through in your story and lend it credibility. Experts and authorities are influential, but personal experience also makes you an influencer. Every single one of the authors mentioned in this book is an expert and an authority. Even those who compiled their information based on interviews and data gathered by others are considered "research experts."

Transformational books also reflect the author's passion and purpose, and they strike an emotional chord in readers. For all these reasons, their written words move reader to action. Keep these characteristics in mind as you develop your detailed outline and begin writing your manuscript.

Writing craft comes into play as well; of course, the book must be well written. Beyond skill in writing nonfiction, fiction, or memoir, employ strategies that help you write a book that creates change. To accomplish this goal, use the following craft-related tips to increase the likelihood of your book inspiring and motivating change.

- **Use persuasive language patterns**—Learn at least the basics of NLP (neuro-linguistic programing), which helps you better understand the way the brain processes the words we use and how that can impact our past, present, and future. There are many NLP language patterns, but with a little knowledge, you can begin using them to move your readers toward change. For example, you might write, "What becomes possible if...?" "You may already know this, but..." or "If you want..., then you...." Additionally, Milton

Erickson's hypnotic language patterns can prove useful. These are often used in marketing copy to get people to take an action, like clicking on a "buy" button. These language patterns include simple phrases like, "Eventually you're going to..." or "When you click on the link, you'll discover..." These simple phrases can have a profound impact on the reader. Shonda Rhimes' *A Year of Yes* is filled with NLP language patterns. And Marianne Williamson's famous passage from *A Return to Love* is a good example, too: "Our deepest fear is not that we are inadequate, it is that we are powerful beyond measure." Also, the line "Actually, who are you not to be?" is an NLP language pattern. Some writers use a few of these patterns naturally. Those who write marketing copy are adept at including them and know how impactful their writing becomes if they do.

- **Create contrast**—Remind your reader, "You are here but want to be there," or "The world is this way, but you want it to be that way." Show them the choices, opportunities, and possibilities available. Raise their ambitions for a better future but also ask them to see the deficits of the present.

- **Demonstrate understanding and expertise**—Share information that demonstrates that you are an expert. Tell stories that illuminate the fact that you have been where they are and understand what it is like, but have found a way to get where they want to go.

- **Offer a clear plan**—If you are writing nonfiction, include specific steps or ways to accomplish change. This helps readers believe they can do it, thereby reducing resistance. If you are writing in a different genre, craft your story around the steps characters take that result in transformation.

- **Tap into emotions**—Use examples that help readers feel change is possible. Increase their desire to change by making them feel uncomfortable staying in their current situation. Show them the consequences of not changing and how that directly impacts them, their lives, their families, or the world. Activate their senses by describing what change looks, feels, smells, tastes, and sounds like. Help them believe they can make a difference. Ask them to imagine what life will be like if they change—or if they don't.

- **Paint a picture**—Use analogy, metaphor, allegory, and descriptive language to stress change's benefits. Ask them to imagine or visualize life after transformation. Tell more stories! Metaphor is often used by writers who understand NLP.
- **Make them the hero**—Base your book on the Hero's Journey. This familiar narrative story template involves a hero who goes on an adventure, meets a guide, learns a lesson, wins a victory, and returns home transformed. Demonstrate how readers can be heroes. Be their guide. Even a nonfiction writer can apply this template by instilling in readers the belief that they can make a difference.

Congratulations! You've done all the preparation work necessary to write a transformational book. You've created a writing guide. You've honed your idea to fit your audience's needs and ensure it is a unique offering in the bookstore category where it will be sold. And you've chosen models, studied the competition, and learned how to write for change.

Now it's time to compose your manuscript. For some people, writing is the fun and easy part. For others, not so much. That's why the next chapter offers tips and strategies to help anyone write effectively, consistently, enthusiastically, and joyously.

10

WRITE A BOOK THAT
MAKES A DIFFERENCE

"In order to write the book you want to write, in the end, you have to become the person you need to become to write that book."

— JUNOT DIAZ

Your long-term success as an Author of Change depends upon your ability to write your transformational book. In 2002, a *New York Times* article stated that 80 percent of all Americans want to write a book; more recently, experts raised the number to 83 percent. Yet only about three percent of those who start writing a book complete the manuscript. Even fewer publish their work. To make your difference in the world as an author and transformational catalyst, you can't let that happen—nor need it happen. You must start and finish your book manuscript if you want to author change.

To write productively and consistently, you may need to adopt strategies, mindsets, and habits that help you complete a manuscript with focus, effectiveness, passion, and inspiration. In other words, you might need to change to become a writer. Take on the identity of "writer" and you'll find it easy to do the things necessary to become an Author of Change, including writing consistently and productively.

Many writers waste time staring at the empty page and wondering what to write. You have created a tool that helps you avoid this condition: You have a three-part writing guide that consists of your purpose statement(s), table of contents, and chapter outline. These elements guide you from the first sentence of your manuscript to the last.

However, your guide is not enough to keep you writing consistently and productively. You also must develop a writing habit and productive writing strategies.

Develop a Writing Habit

Many aspiring writers —and even many seasoned authors— struggle to write consistently. Career writers treat writing as a job, sitting down at the computer Monday through Friday and churning out "work." For them, writing has become an automatic behavior—a habit. Studies show that it can take sixty-six days or more to develop a habit of any kind. That means you must commit to writing at least five days per week for three months to develop a writing habit. If you write less than this, you'll struggle to develop this automatic behavior, and writing daily will remain something you think about but don't always do. It will continue to be a daily decision—write, or don't write?—rather than something you do without question.

There's no guarantee that three months of writing will result in the formation of a habit. The same studies show that habit formation takes more than two hundred days for some people. That's six months of writing practice before you get down to writing each day as a matter of course—like brushing your teeth, making coffee, or putting on socks. You want writing to become a rote behavior, too—with no wondering if you should or will write today, instead sitting down to write...no matter what...because it is your habit.

Developing a writing habit begins with planning. Get out your calendar, planner, or scheduling app, and make writing appointments with yourself. Approach these blocks of writing time on your weekly schedule as non-negotiable meetings which you must attend. To help make that happen, behavioral scientist B.J. Fogg recommends attaching your new habit—blocks of writing time—to an already established habit. For instance, if you shower, dress, and make coffee —in that order—every morning, writing could fit nicely into your routine after making coffee. Take the steamy mug to your office and start writing.

Additionally, Fogg recommends starting with "tiny habits" that don't feel overwhelming. For instance, instead of planning to write for two hours when you typically don't write at all, write for thirty minutes. Grow into longer time blocks. You can even start with fifteen-minute writing blocks for a week or two, then thirty minutes for two weeks, and then forty-five minutes for two more weeks. When you write easily and consistently for three quarters of an hour, increase your writing time again to sixty minutes, ninety minutes, and then two hours—or longer.

Your body has a natural rhythm that makes it easy to be productive at certain times of the day and unproductive at others; the study of these rhythms is called chronobiology. Learn your body's natural rhythms—when you find it easy to focus and accomplish tasks and when you feel more distracted and less productive. Track your productivity for a week or two and determine your most productive times of day; then, if possible, schedule your writing blocks during those periods. Save more mindless tasks for your least productive times of day, and you'll eliminate some of the struggle involved in establishing a writing habit.

If you can't write during your most productive time of day, find ways to energize yourself so you learn to be more focused and effective during your off times. I teach my clients a four-part ritual to do before writing to help them get focused and energized before they write—even if they are tired, overwhelmed, or distracted coming into the writing session. Here are the four steps:

- **Meditate for two minutes.** Start with three deep breaths, in through the nose and out through the mouth. Then, focus on your breath, be mindful of your surroundings, or use a mantra like, "I am here" or, as Burchard recommends, "Release." This process allows you to become present and let go of any mental clutter that might distract you.
- **Set an intention.** Clearly state (in your mind or aloud) your intention for the writing session. What do you want to accomplish? For example, your goal might be to complete the next two sections of Chapter 4 or to write five hundred words. You now have a target to hit, which will keep you moving toward it.
- **Breathe.** Stand up. Breathing in and out through the nose, complete twenty forceful, deep, rapid diaphragmatic breaths, clapping your hands on each exhale. These breaths should cause your abdomen, not your chest, to rise. Do not breath so forcefully or quickly that you feel dizzy. You should feel energized afterward—even tingly. This process oxygenates your body and brain, causing your tiredness and distraction to fall away and leaving you ready to write.
- **Repeat a trigger word or phrase.** After you complete the twenty breaths, clap five more times while saying, "I'm ready," "I've got this," "I can write," "Write!" or whatever word or phrase you choose. Get increasingly louder with each repetition. Used regularly, a trigger word creates a neural pathway in your brain. Like a habit, over time, when your brain hears the word or phrase, it knows it's time to

write productively. It will help you get down to business quickly (even without the breathing)!

Habits are routines—we repeat them regularly and without thought. However, if you turn routines into rituals, they hold greater meaning. Specifically, writing rituals helps you connect to your reasons for writing and align with your purpose. Consider creating a writing ritual, such as meditating or journaling, lighting a candle or saying a prayer, energetically clearing your space with incense or sage, or reciting your purpose statement aloud before you begin writing. Rituals set the mood for writing and create a sacred space in which to write. They also serve as writing triggers. Your writing becomes part of the ritual—or a habit tacked onto the ritual habit.

Consider your environment as well. You'll find it easier to write in a space conducive to creative work. You might want the space to have a spiritual or sacred quality, in which case place crystals and candles or a picture of a spiritual leader on your desk. You can even place a photo of a writer whom you consider a role model within sight.

It's easy for your writing space to get cluttered and messy. Tidy up each evening to prepare the space for the next day of writing. Remove physical distractions, including chaotic piles of papers, so it is easier to get into the flow the next time you sit down to write. Also, check your book outline to ensure you know what you need to write next. Then, you won't waste time figuring this out at the start of the writing block.

In your journal, describe the type of writing ritual you would find most meaningful and useful. Also, plan how to create an inspiring and sacred writing space. Additionally, consider what type of trigger might help you get into the writing zone quickly and how you might use it. Last, get out your planner or calendar and block out your writing times.

Create a Positive and Productive Mindset

Mindset is a habit. You habitually think certain thoughts that influence how you see yourself, others, the world, and your writing project. According to the National Science Foundation, an average person has about twelve thousand to sixty thousand thoughts per day—that's between five hundred and two thousand five hundred thoughts per hour. (Other experts report we might think as many as eighty thousand thoughts per day.) Of those thoughts, the majority are subconscious; we don't know we are thinking them.

Your mind is like an iceberg. Ninety percent of an iceberg hides beneath the surface of the water, while only about 10 percent is visible above the water level. Neuroscientists at Stanford, Harvard, MIT, and other institutions have determined that the human brain operates in a similar fashion. Like an iceberg, your mind has conscious thoughts that are visible above the water line—which represent only 10 percent of your total brain function. But most of your mental activity is subconscious thoughts—90 percent of your total brain function—that lie hidden below the surface.

Conscious vs. Unconscious Thoughts

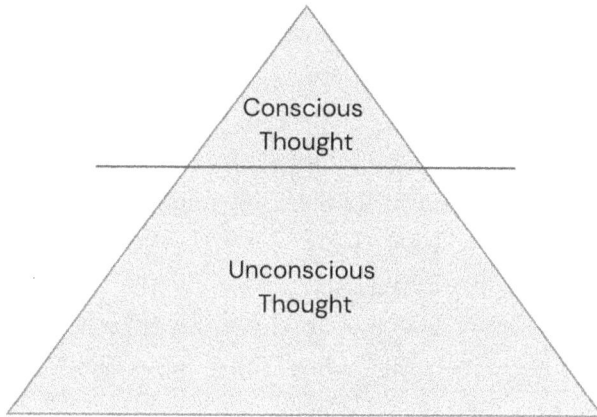

Conscious
Thought

Unconscious
Thought

Additionally, 80 percent of your thoughts are negative and 95 percent are repetitive. If you repeat negative thoughts frequently, you develop negative beliefs and a negative mindset. The more positive thoughts you think, the more positive your beliefs and mindset. If you've ever found yourself in a funk, you know how negative thoughts—along with the resulting negative emotions and sapped energy—make productivity difficult.

A negative mindset also makes it hard to write and publish a book. In this frame of mind, you're likely to think, "I'm not good enough," "I have nothing to write that is worth reading," "No one will buy my book, so why bother?" "I can't do this," or "This is too hard." Your negative mental self-talk leads to negative emotions, and you feel defeated before you begin. If you start working on your book, you might feel overwhelmed and unable to do the work needed to finish it. Your negative thoughts and emotions may affect your energy, making you tired and lethargic. You probably realize a negative mindset can cause you to give up before you complete—or even start —a book project.

On the other hand, the more positive your mindset, the more likely you are to succeed. Dr. Martin E.P. Seligman, the father of Positive Psychology, found that positive people aren't put off by criticism, rejection, and initial failure. They keep telling themselves they are on the right track and therefore succeed. While this may sometimes seem unrealistic, it keeps them moving toward their goal. They don't get stuck as often, partially because they don't take setbacks personally and look for new ways to improve their efforts. Negative people convince themselves setbacks are personal—they or their work are at fault or somehow below par. So, they quit. Their negative mindset lowers their tenacity level, while those who develop a positive mindset increase their tenacity level.

Developing a more positive mindset also increases your level of productivity. In 1998 and 2000, a landmark study by B.L. Frederickson found that positivity increases focus and cognitive ability. Negativity decreases the very things you need to be productive, such as the optimal functioning of your prefrontal cortex, an area of the brain critical for creativity, decision-making, and seeing solutions. Also, negativity creates chronic stress, which causes inflammation throughout the body and leads to ill health. When you are battling health problems—even the common cold—it's hard to write or pursue success as an author, change agent, or leader. Additionally, negativity won't help you attract people to your cause. Few people want to engage with someone who is pessimistic. Positivity, on the other hand, is attractive and magnetically draws an audience to you.

This same study by Frederickson demonstrated that positivity increases risk tolerance. Setting out to become an author—let alone an Author of Change—represents a risky venture. It takes courage to put yourself and your beliefs out into the world not knowing how either will be received. Plus, becoming an author involves a personal investment of both money and time with little assured return; but your positive mindset will help you courageously write your book and create change in the world.

Ultimately, a positive mindset helps you achieve success. What you think is what you get. Think positive thoughts, get positive results. Energetically, the more positive your mindset, the more positive you feel and the more positive energy you put out into the world, which helps you attract more readers and have more impact.

How to Focus on Writing Rather than Distractions

Distractions are the enemy of productivity. Learn to reduce or eliminate whatever takes your attention away from writing. Distractions might be your personal social media account, email, children, pets, laundry, or dirty dishes. Or your focus might be stolen by the need to promote your cause, build your author platform, create a website, submit query letters to agents, or find a manuscript editor.

Whatever your brand of distraction, I've found a solution that works: Relegate that activity to a block of time in your schedule that is separate from writing time. On your calendar or in your planner, create time blocks for your personal social media account, email, laundry, walking the dog, or finding an editor, for example. Don't do any of those tasks during your writing blocks—not even revising or editing, which should have time blocks of their own.

Many writers get distracted by the need to build an engaged audience, and their platform-building activities end up taking precedence over writing. For instance, once they turn their attention to Instagram to increase audience size, they get sucked into looking at new posts and stories. Don't let that be you! Instead, see your time on social networks as work—not pleasure—and be businesslike about it. Compartmentalize all community building activities. Get in, do what you must do, and get out. Come back later to socialize as a reward for having written.

Procrastination, which is a result of resistance, often looks like giving in to distraction, which I discuss later in this chapter. It's easy to find other things to do when you are consciously or subconsciously avoiding writing. So, become aware of how you procrastinate—eating, scrolling through social media posts, folding laundry, or feeding the birds—and eliminate anything possible that allows you to avoid writing. This can take the form of folding the laundry and feeding the birds in the evening so these tasks are not on your mind the next morning when you sit down to write. Eliminating distractions can also look like eating before you write so you have no reason to get up and look for snacks during your writing block, or turning off your cell phone and your Internet connection during a writing block so you can't access any social media sites. Once you have eliminated distractions, sit your butt in the chair and write! (But don't use elimination of distractions as a distraction! Yes, that's a thing.)

Goal setting provides an effective way to keep yourself writing. For example, set a goal to write daily from 10 to 12 a.m. or to complete five hundred words of your manuscript daily. (Eventually, that will become a habit!) Or set a goal to finish a chapter of your book every week, or the first draft of your book in six months and the second draft three months later. Goals increase your sense of urgency and necessity, making it highly likely you stay focused on writing.

A big-picture view of your project serves the same purpose. Let's say you want to self-publish your book by January 1. You can create a set of mini deadlines based on meeting that final deadline. Remind yourself of the production schedule for your book, and you'll be more likely to be consistently focused and productive. The same is true if you traditionally publish. The publisher provides a production schedule that includes each deadline along the way—submission of the final manuscript, receipt of editor's comments, return of manuscript with changes, proofreading, submission of foreword and testimonials, and release date. With that final date and the deadlines that must be met in between firmly in mind, you feel the necessity of writing every day.

Productive Writing Strategies

Based on my experience as a writer, author, author coach, transformational coach, and Certified High Performance Coach, here are a few additional strategies to help you write productively.

Avoid Overwhelm

Overwhelm leads to procrastination. When I feel overwhelmed, I find numerous things to do instead of writing. When a deadline looms, my lack of productivity makes me feel more overwhelmed. It's a vicious cycle. To avoid overwhelm, try the following:

- **Create realistic and manageable deadlines.** Work backward from a deadline to determine how much time you need to meet it. For instance, if you know you must submit your final manuscript by November 10, do not set July 10 as the start date for writing your book. You may need more than five months to finish your manuscript. And give yourself a grace period: Decide to complete the manuscript a month early. Then use that month to polish your prose one final time.

  Also, knowing how many words you write per hour helps determine the amount of time you need to produce a 50,000-word manuscript, as an example. Schedule research time, which is a separate writing-related task that should be scheduled in a different time block. And always overestimate the time you need to meet your deadline.

- **Hire help.** A sure-fire way to reduce overwhelm is to get help. Assistance could be anything from a babysitter to a virtual assistant to a transcriber. It could look like your husband watching the kids for two hours while you write, your neighbor handling the carpool for you, or your friends agreeing to bring over dinners the last two weeks of your deadline. Or perhaps help might mean finding a housekeeper or dog walker.

- **Take mini vacations.** It's easy to get burned out if you have no time away from the computer or your daily responsibilities. If you start feeling burned out, you'll struggle to write productively. So, find a day each week or every month to do absolutely nothing. Take care of yourself. Consider this a mini vacation—a day at the beach, reading a novel, visiting friends or family, or going for a long hike. You'll come back to your manuscript more focused, creative, and productive.

- **Manage your schedule.** Block out time for a task, like writing, and use that time to complete that task. Be strict with yourself. The more disciplined you are about your schedule, the more freedom you'll have to do other things— like building your community, spending time with family members, or relaxing—all of which should have scheduled time blocks.

Get—and Stay—Organized

Organization is key to writing productively. This is not my forte, but while writing a book, I'm super vigilant about getting and staying organized. Spending lots of time looking for your research, the last version of a chapter, a pen, or a sticky note leaves little time to write.

First, organize your manuscript. This might mean creating a primary book folder using Google Drive, Microsoft Word, or Scrivener, unless you prefer physical folders in a filing cabinet. Add chapter folders or files to this folder. Some writers save chapter documents with the chapter title and date included in the file name to avoid confusion about which is the most recent document. Others create folders for most recent or final drafts. Find a system that works for you.

Second, organize your research. Let's start with online research. Avoid losing research you find on the Internet by creating a system for saving useful sites, articles, or blog posts. You can do this in your Internet Browser by *bookmarking* pages as well as saving them in a browser folder. Scrivener allows you to drag links into the research area of your book "binder." Organize those links by chapter. Evernote has a great "web clipper" feature as well, and you can tag research to simplify locating it later, or you can place it in "notebooks." Or create a research folder on your computer in a text editing application like Word, Pages, or Google Drive. Copy and paste research, including links to online articles, into files and save them to the folder.

If you prefer physical research—books, magazine and newspaper articles, and printouts of online research results—an organizational system becomes essential. Don't let your newly cleaned and organized space become cluttered with research piles. Your system might include putting papers in folders in a filing cabinet or organizing your book with hanging folders for each chapter. Or you might get a plastic box that holds hanging folders and use this to organize your book project.

Only Write

If you have scheduled a block of time for writing, only write during that period. Don't do anything else; this includes research and revision. As soon as you allow yourself to begin editing your work, you call in the critical part of your brain. While the Inner Critic provides a useful service while editing and revising, it hinders your writing progress by causing you to question every word. It's the internal voice that says, "It's not good enough." "You're a lousy writer." "That sentence isn't grammatically correct." "You can find a better word than that one." This type of self-talk lowers your creativity and confidence when writing, although it proves helpful when working on additional manuscript drafts.

The same goes for research. Research requires the brain to analyze material. The more you analyze, the less creativity you experience. Plus, research is a sinkhole; it's easy to fall into and hard to climb out. You might tell yourself you need just one more bit of research—a statistic, for instance—before you can continue writing. But by the time you get back to your manuscript, two hours have passed, and you've run out of writing time. To avoid these issues, each time you come across a need for research while writing, type the word "research" in brackets. You might even include the type of research you need, like this: [research—statistics on how many people currently compost] or [research—number of people globally who are introverts]. Later, during a research time block, search your document for the word "research" and locate the information needed. Then, during a writing period, write those sections of your manuscript; or block out time for adding research.

Take Frequent Breaks

Many writers think it takes time to get in the flow. Once they get into that state, they become unwilling to take a break. In fact, frequent breaks keep you productive and creative. As it turns out, humans are not built to concentrate for hours on end. That's why they are on average productive for only three hours of a normal eight-hour workday. A study from the University of Illinois confirms that your performance declines if you must focus on a single task for a long time. When you don't take breaks, you may suffer from decision fatigue, lack of focus, and eye issues. However, behavioral scientist Nir Eyal explains that breaks can reduce mental fatigue, boost brain function, and help you remain focused.

According to research from the University of Southern California, your brain uses breaks to make important connections that help you recall personal memories—important if you are writing a memoir, for instance. When writing a book, taking short regular breaks can:

1. Help you make better decisions
2. Spark creative ideas and solutions
3. Allow you to stay focused longer
4. Improve your retention of information
5. Support your ability to recall stories more easily

A break can provide the lightbulb moment you need. That's why so many writers claim they do more writing while taking a short walk than during time spent at their desks. Your brain works on problems when you aren't focused on them. Therefore, getting away from the computer for ten or fifteen minutes for a short run, a shower, or to pick flowers in your garden can lead to a new idea or a solution to a writing problem.

In the world of high performance, the gold standard is a five or ten-minute break every fifty minutes. This correlates with the University of Illinois study, which suggests taking a break once per hour. However, some people find this period too short. Tony Schwartz, the author of *The Power of Full Engagement*, found that humans tend to move from full focus to fatigue every ninety minutes, which explains why many people prefer to take a break about an hour and a half after they begin work. The Pomodoro Technique, a popular productivity strategy, promotes taking a three-to-five-minute break every twenty-five minutes or a fifteen-to-thirty-minute break every ninety minutes. Chronobiology plays into break time as well. If you get drowsy at 2 p.m. every afternoon, that's a good time for your afternoon nap! Try different intervals to discover what works best for you.

During writing breaks, participate in activities that enhance your ability to write. Do something that is mindless but gives your brain what it needs for optimal function—air, water, and nutrients. Also move your body, which is not meant to sit still for long periods of time. You might:

- Meditate for five minutes.
- Do breathing exercises
- Stretch, or do yoga or tai chi
- Drink water
- Have a healthy snack
- Take supplements

Manage Your Energy

Breaks that involve the types of activities mentioned above help you manage your energy, too. Three types of energy affect your ability to write: mental, physical, and emotional.

If your mental energy wanes, such as when you've written for three hours straight, you'll have a hard time continuing to work productively. That's where breaks and feeding your brain what it needs to function come into play.

If your physical energy drops, your brain also loses the power it needs to concentrate and work effectively. To write productively, sleep enough, exercise, eat well, and generally take care of your health. A big hamburger right before you sit down to write may leave you lethargic and sleepy while a salad with healthy protein could boost your energy.

If your emotional energy ranges from high to low, your ability to write follows suit. When you are sad or depressed, your physical and mental energy decrease. If you are infatuated or excited, your overly high energy may make it hard to sit down, be still, and focus. Your emotions are closely tied to your thoughts. If your thoughts are focused on negativity, your emotional state becomes negative, and your body responds with low energy. Of course, the opposite is true as well—positive thoughts lead to positive emotions and higher energy.

Manage your energy level consistently, and you'll find yourself more able to write effectively, productively, and creatively.

Don't Let Life Get in the Way

The most common excuse I hear from people who aren't writing—but say they want to do so—is that "life got in the way." Indeed, life has a way of happening despite our best efforts to control it. Given that life always happens—usually at inopportune or inconvenient times—develop a strategy for prioritizing writing no matter your life circumstances.

There will be times when you legitimately have to drop your writing schedule to deal with life; for example, when there is a death in the family or you experience a health crisis. Most other situations that arise—like children getting sick, the car breaking down, or betrayal by a friend or lover—do not have to get in the way of writing.

If you are committed to your book and authoring change, make writing a priority, and have learned to govern your mindset and developed a habit and ritual around writing, you can write no matter what life throws your way. It's always possible to get in fifteen to thirty minutes of writing—even if it means waking up earlier, going to bed later, or writing during your lunch hour, for instance. If you allow your mind to focus on life issues, however, you'll struggle to place attention on your book manuscript.

Do whatever you can to maintain your momentum and stay engaged in relationship with your book project. It's amazing how one week without writing turns into two or three...or more, disconnecting you from the project as a result. When that happens, you need to reacquaint yourself with the manuscript, a time-consuming process that involves rereading your work. Avoid this by writing daily, even for very brief periods. In situations where you don't have the mental capacity to write, revise—even just one paragraph, because doing so connects you to the work until you can find the mental bandwidth to write.

It's enormously useful to create an "if this, then that" strategy for life's common occurrences. For example, if your child, dog, or spouse becomes ill or you get the flu, what will you do to ensure you still write? The "if" in this example equates to "illness." Your strategy in response to such a situation—the action you will take when it arises —is something to consider in advance. You could adopt the strategy, "If someone in my care gets sick, then I will write while they nap," or "If I get sick, I will make up the writing blocks on subsequent weekends." You can create an emergency plan that keeps you writing for almost any "if" situation. I've known people who wrote while hospitalized or by the bedside of an ill child and took their laptops on vacation.

In your journal, explore strategies you can employ to ensure "life" doesn't get in the way of your writing. Consider every scenario, excuse, or reason you might have for not writing, and create strategies for each one.

Getting Past the Tough Times

Inevitably, you will encounter times when writing your book feels challenging. Even seasoned writers admit to such experiences. The difference between those who succeed and those who don't, however, depends upon the writers' ability to forge on—even when they think they can't. You might find it difficult to write through the middle of your book, to work through editors' revisions or self-edit your manuscript, to cope with agent or publisher rejections, or to get past your self-criticism and self-doubt. All of this is normal. However, at these times, you must remain committed to your purpose—authoring change.

In *The War of Art*, Steven Pressfield discusses how to overcome the enemy—resistance. He says you need a battle plan to conquer this internal foe. He would know. It took him seventeen years to earn any money from writing, twenty-seven years to publish his first novel, and fifty years to make a living from his words. Pressfield describes resistance as a negative force that keeps you from fulfilling your dreams. Resistance can show up as worry that you don't have enough talent, that you won't have the time or money to complete your book project, or that you will be judged once your book is published. Pressfield claims overcoming resistance is more important than talent, because many people have talent but few put in the work to realize it. Or they allow self-doubt, procrastination, or self-sabotage to hold them back.

How do you overcome resistance? Pressfield suggests the following:

1. ***When you work—work.*** Writing time is writing time—
   even when you find it hard to write. In *The War of Art*,
   Pressfield explains that it doesn't matter to him how much
   or how well he writes each day. "All that matters is that I've
   put in my time and hit the wall with all I've got. All that

counts is, for this day, for this session, I have overcome Resistance."

2. ***Turn pro and don't look back.*** You may have your own definition of what it means to "turn pro," or you might think it's a title bestowed upon you, like by a coach when an athlete gets drafted to a pro team. That's not the case with writers—at least not as Pressfield describes it. Instead, turning pro is a deliberate and powerful decision to become a professional in anything you do, but in this case, it means you adopt a professional writing mindset. Pros don't allow resistance to get in the way of success; they write despite resistance. I've always loved this quotation from Somerset Maugham, which applies here. When asked if he wrote on a schedule or only when struck by inspiration, Maugham responded, "I write only when inspiration strikes. Fortunately, it strikes every morning at nine o'clock sharp." Create your ritual, habit, and writing schedule. Inspiration will strike each time you sit down to write, too.

3. ***Change happens now.*** Time to revisit personal change and the creation of new, supportive habits. One of the biggest forms of resistance is habitual procrastination, Pressfield explains. "We don't put off our lives today; we put them off till our deathbed. Never forget: This very moment, we can change our lives. There never was a moment, and never will be, when we are without the power to alter our destiny." Become an Author of Change by taking charge of your destiny and refusing to allow resistance of any sort— including procrastination—to kill your dream. Take action. The best way to move through resistance is to start writing.

4. ***Become who you already are.*** Who are you at your core? It's likely you are a change maker. And it's highly likely you are a writer—or that you can choose to be one. "We come into this world with a specific, personal destiny," writes Pressfield. "We have a job to do, a calling to enact,

a self to become." When you combine who you are with who you want to become, you overcome resistance. You do things that align with that identity—like creating change or writing a book that makes a difference. Pressfield points out that resistance can appear as the kind of self-talk that echoes Williamson's quote, "Who am I to think I can be an Author of Change?" Who are you not to be that—if that is the identity you choose? Know who you are and become the highest and best possible version of yourself. Choose to be a committed, productive, tenacious writer and Author of Change. Take on those identities.

You are on a Hero's Journey. You will come to a point while writing your transformational book where you will encounter tests, allies, enemies (like resistance), and ordeals—challenges that make it feel impossible to continue writing. At that point, it's useful to use Pressfield's advice or look for other resources—and even guides—to support your journey. For instance, seek out a book or author coach, a critique group, or a writing partner. Go to a writing conference, hire an editor, or find an accountability buddy.

Getting Through Revisions and Rejection

In addition to resistance, two other "Rs" may show up as obstacles to writing and publishing your work—revisions and rejection. When you or an editor read your manuscript with an eye for what still needs to be corrected, that's editing. Typically, a developmental editor looks at a manuscript first with an eye for big-picture issues; do the same yourself before hiring an editor. Both of you will look for issues like redundancies, unanswered questions, and misplaced content. Then, you go through a revision process to correct the issues. Some writers revise soon after completing a section or chapter, but a full read-through of the manuscript makes revision more effective.

Some people enjoy revisions; for them, rewriting, moving content, answering questions, and deleting unnecessary words and paragraphs feels easier than writing from scratch. For others, however, revision is drudgery—especially when you must do it more than once. Discovering manuscript issues can feel overwhelming or bring up negative self-talk about your ability to produce a good and marketable book. Self-criticism, overwhelm, and the need to painstakingly make changes to your work can lead back to the first "R"—resistance.

To avoid resistance during the revision process, keep your purpose in mind. You want to author change and produce the best possible manuscript. Direct your Inner Critic—the voice saying your manuscript is horrible and you can't write—toward improving your work. It's a great editor! The revision process is the perfect time to ask your critical brain functions to take part in the process.

If you continue to feel resistance to reworking your manuscript, revise in short blocks of time, alternating revision with other tasks you enjoy. I suggest revising a specific number of pages every day. Break your manuscript into bite-sized pieces. For instance, if your first draft is 50,000 words, or about two hundred fifty double-spaced pages, set a goal of revising fifty pages per week, or ten pages per day (working Monday through Friday). This strategy helps you move forward steadily and build momentum.

If you feel resistance to reading and editing your first draft, use the same strategy. Choose how many pages you will read per week or per day. Set aside time daily for this task and work consistently. Your progress gives you confidence.

Another aspect of revision involves line editing, which is also sometimes called copy editing. Such editors look at sentence-level issues like structure, punctuation, and grammar. Line editing is painstaking work. After developmental editing, turn your attention to your sentences; make them as strong, tight, and compelling as possible. Use the same strategies already mentioned to get through this process without resistance. Block time, put your Inner Critic to good use, set deadlines and quotas, and reward yourself for meeting them. When you are done, hire a line editor—someone with fresh eyes—for a final manuscript polish.

The third "R" is rejection, and it, too, can cause resistance. I know this well. For years, I didn't let rejections of my query letters or book proposals stop me. With each rejection, I said, "Next!" I reminded myself of author Jack Canfield's advice: After each rejection, say, "I must have sent this to the wrong person. Next time, I'll send it to the right one."

Then, I found myself faced with a huge opportunity to pitch to a publisher. A rejection followed, but it came with an offer to meet with several editors from the publishing house to discuss other potential projects along with my agent. After producing a second proposal, I was again rejected. I lost my confidence and mojo; I resisted writing my next book proposal...and writing that book—*this* one. I had produced two book proposals in less than a year, but this one ended up taking me a year to produce. The writing of this book felt harder after the disappointment of that rejection, and it took me seven years to complete the final manuscript.

In my late twenties and early thirties, I was involved with the Loving Relationships Training, a personal growth program created by Sondra Ray. There I learned about the Rejection Quota—another strategy I use when in the submission process. When you receive rejection letters from literary agents or publishers, reframe this experience. Remind yourself that you have not yet met your rejection quota. Continue sending out queries and proposals. When you have met your quota, you will get an acceptance—maybe even more than one.

Some change agents and writers never start their manuscripts, or if they do, they don't finish them. They are so afraid of rejection in its many forms that they avoid potentially encountering this undesirable experience. That, too, is a form of resistance. Keep your purpose at the forefront of all you do. Remind yourself that someone out there needs your book—now. Necessity then keeps you writing and submitting your manuscript—for your readers.

With all of this in mind, get out your journal and answer the following questions:

- What's your biggest challenge when it comes to writing your manuscript's first draft? How can you overcome it?
- Do you enjoy editing and revising your work? If not, how can you make these tasks more enjoyable or make this task palatable?
- What negative thoughts do you have about writing your book? What positive affirmations can you adopt instead?
- What causes you the most resistance to writing consistently or editing and revising? How will you destroy this "enemy"?
- What are your common excuses for not writing? (You may dub these "reasons.")

Pace Yourself

Finally, if you want to write consistently, pace yourself. Sometimes, all you will want to do is write. You may get up at 5 a.m. inspired to get to the computer. In a flow state, you may write without eating or drinking, only getting up from your desk for bathroom breaks. Then, late in the evening, you feel drained. The next day, despite your desire to write, you're too exhausted. Obviously, you can't write consistently with this type of process.

Set a reasonable pace for yourself. Decide how much time daily you will spend writing. Stick to your schedule. Remember that you will be more productive and creative if you take breaks.

The tortoise won the race, right? Behave like the hare, and you'll eventually fall behind. However, if you combine the tenacity and endurance of the tortoise with the speed of the hare, you will get to your destination—successful authorship—with grace and ease. Recall that the tortoise didn't stop. Stopping not only slows your progress but may also result in your never getting back in the race.

Sometimes you may feel an internal push to write...and write a lot. I'm not telling you to ignore your calling, inspiration, motivation, or the ability to get into a peak state and produce tons of content quickly. I'm cautioning you not to do that consistently. Instead, force yourself to take breaks—even if that means you must set a timer or alarm. Make yourself eat, drink, and move on your breaks; give your body and mind what they need to help you write. And don't write for more than eight hours per day. Allow yourself to rest so you can write the next day, and the next, and so on.

Allow writing your book to generate the energy needed to complete the project. After all, the finished manuscript—and published book —are how you make a positive and meaningful difference with your words. They are how you become an Author of Change.

In the conclusion that follows, we will take a brief look at the final step to authoring change—publishing.

CONCLUSION:
TIME FOR ACTION

"You are not obligated to complete the work, but neither are you free to desist from it."

— RABBI TARFON

I f you want to author change, you must take action...more action than simply writing a manuscript. It's imperative that you not only take to heart all that you've learned in this book but use that knowledge and act on it.

Also, you must transform yourself from a writer into an author. Remember: An author is a writer who has published their written work. An Author of Change has published a transformational book with the potential to change the world...one reader at a time.

Publish Your Book

A completed manuscript is worth celebrating; it's a huge accomplishment and a gigantic step toward authoring change. However, until you turn that manuscript into a book, it won't help you make a difference. To fulfill your purpose and your book's purpose, your next action step requires publishing your manuscript.

The United Nations Educational, Scientific and Cultural Organization (UNESCO) estimates that 2.2 million books are published every year. If you recall, few writers complete book manuscripts; of those that do, even fewer publish them. Traditional publishing continues to become ever more competitive, with only one percent (or less) of writers landing a contract. Anyone can self-publish, but many writers bail when they realize the costs and tasks involved. Others get stumped by self-publishing technicalities or become too overwhelmed—and afraid— to choose a self-publishing strategy. For this reason, many aspiring authors remain unpublished.

You, however, have a cause to support and a mission to pursue. You are committed to achieving your purpose and that of your book. Allowing your manuscript to sit unread in a computer file is not an option. So, raise the bar on your commitment and willingness to do whatever it takes to publish. Marketer extraordinaire Seth Godin says, "The only purpose of starting is to finish, and while the projects we do are never really finished, they must ship."

It's time to "ship" your book! Get it into the hands of readers.

Whether you have dreamed of becoming published traditionally, want to self-publish, or are considering a hybrid path, it's important to understand and weigh your options and make an informed decision about which is best for you and your book. Many books teach publishing options, including my book, *The Author Training Manual*. So, I will keep this discussion brief.

You have three distinct publishing options:

1. Self-publishing (author pays for everything and makes all decisions)
2. Traditional publishing (publisher pays for everything and makes all decisions)
3. Hybrid publishing (author pays and works with a publisher in making decisions)

All too often I hear aspiring authors talk about self-publishing as if it is *the* way to produce a book. They want control over this final step, a larger percentage of income from sales, the ability to quickly bring a book to market, and the freedom of not having to get past gatekeepers. However, some of these writers don't realize that self-publishing requires becoming a publisher and tackling the tasks included in that job description. Additionally, self-publishing can be the most expensive path in terms of time and money. (Warning: There are many so-called self-publishing options that involve paying a company to edit, design, and manufacture your book. These subsidy publishing companies, formerly called vanity presses, can prove expensive, low quality, and problematic in various other ways. This option is not "true" self-publishing.)

Aspiring authors who think traditional publishing is *the* way to produce a book believe a publisher's backing means their book will succeed. They may mistakenly believe they won't need to promote it upon release and that the book will magically rise to bestseller status. While traditionally published books continue to offer more clout than self-published books and typically are distributed to brick-and-mortar bookstores, getting the support of a publishing house doesn't guarantee success, fame, fortune, or marketing help. These days, it doesn't even mean the offer of a huge advance (or any advance at all).

Plus, in most cases, landing a traditional publishing contract requires finding a literary agent to represent you and your book idea to acquisitions editors at publishing houses. Publishers and acquisitions editors rely on literary agents to vet book ideas and authors. You can pitch small publishers on your own, but most mid-sized and large publishers only accept agented submissions.

To pitch agents or publishers, you need a query letter that answers the following questions: Why this book? Why now? And why you? If your book is nonfiction, you also need to produce a book proposal. Agents and publishers use this "business plan" to determine if your book project is viable. Writing a book proposal can prove a lengthy process, but it's valuable. I recommend even writers who want to self-publish create a book proposal for this reason.

If you plan to publish multiple books, you can become a hybrid author and do so traditionally and independently. This path allows you to utilize the strengths and opportunities of both types of publishing.

Additionally, you can choose to publish with a hybrid publisher. This happy medium between traditional publishers and self-publishing typically involves less of a financial investment (if any). And you won't have to go it alone; you'll have a partner who provides a professional team to get your book into the world. Some hybrid publishers also provide traditional distribution mechanisms.

How do you know which publishing path is right for you and your book? Answer the following questions in your journal to gain clarity and decide.

Traditional Publishing

1. Do you have a solid, marketable book idea?
2. Can you prove your book is both unique and necessary in the bookstore category where it will be sold?
3. Are you telling a story that has never been told or providing new information or strategies?

4. If writing a memoir, are you offering an extraordinary story about an ordinary person?
5. Can you clearly explain your book's concept to an agent and publisher in under two minutes?
6. Will your book concept inspire confidence in an agent and publisher?
7. Can you demonstrate in a proposal your ability to deliver what you promise?
8. If your book is nonfiction, is it prescriptive enough that the agent or editor will see its purpose and value?
9. Have you developed a solid author platform that can be quantified?
10. Are you willing to produce a solid book proposal (business plan) that illustrates that you have a marketable idea and are the best person to develop it into a book?
11. Do you have a clear plan for how to promote your book online and off?
12. Do you feel confident that you can promote your book effectively?
13. Are you willing to let someone edit and suggest how to improve the manuscript?
14. Are you willing to give up control of your vision for your book, including details such as the book title and cover, and allow a team of professionals to make these decisions?
15. Are you willing to put in the time and work to find a literary agent to represent you to publishers?
16. Are you willing to wait for publishing professionals—like agents and acquisitions editors—to respond to your queries and offer you contracts?

If you answered "no" to more than half of these questions, you might not be ready to approach traditional publishers. In fact, you may be better suited to self-publishing. If this is the case, skip the traditional publishing route and take advantage of what self-publishing offers, including immediacy, more direct control, and the chance for greater profit per book sale.

If you answered "yes" to most of the questions, traditional publishing may offer the best route to authorship for you; make it your Plan A. Traditional publishing offers you and your book credibility, an advance (payment) for your work, wider distribution, and a team of professionals to handle the editing and design of your book. If you don't land a traditional publishing deal, you can self-publish instead.

Self-Publishing

- Do you like "project management"?
- Are you detail oriented?
- Are you a good people manager who wants to manage a team to help you publish your book?
- Can you juggle many balls at the same time?
- Do you want control over certain aspects of your book project, such as editing, design, and release date?
- Are you willing and able to invest your own money in your book project?
- Do you want to learn how to publish a book? And do you have the time to do so?
- Do you have the money to hire someone to assist with self-publishing?
- Are you in a hurry to get your book to market?
- Are you entrepreneurial or a good businessperson who wants to run your own publishing company?
- Do you like taking ideas from start to finish?
- Do you have the confidence to take your book from manuscript to published book?
- Do you set deadlines for yourself and keep them?

If you answered "yes" to more than half of these questions, you are cut out to be a self-publisher. If you answered, "yes" to all of them, self-publishing is your clear-cut route. On the other hand, if you answered "no" to more than half of the questions above, consider attempting traditional publishing first; you can pursue self-publishing if that doesn't work out. Or seek a done-for-you service, assisted self-publishing, or hybrid publishing.

The Final Step to Authoring Change

At this point, the only thing left for you to do is take action—become an Author of Change. As you've learned, a transformational book alone can become a magnet for like-minded souls who want to accomplish personal change or create change in the world.

A transformational book leaves a legacy, creating positive and meaningful change for many years after publication. Thus, a movement started today might continue to inspire people well into the future.

As I said in this book's introduction, the world needs repair. It's not up to you to complete all the repair, but you can begin fixing what needs to be fixed by understanding how people change, creating a community of people interested in your brand of change, and writing and publishing a book that can change the world.

That's my challenge to you.

Repair the world by writing and publishing a book that makes a difference! Now, go author change.

ACKNOWLEDGMENTS

I would like to acknowledge Brenda Knight, publisher of Books that Save Lives, for believing in me and this book. She made it possible for my words to make a positive and meaningful difference in the world and to ripple out and help other writers do the same.

Also, I would like to thank Michael Larsen, who invited me to speak at the San Francisco Writing for Change Conference and, later, encouraged me to write a book that supports aspiring authors writing for change.

Last, but not least, I want to acknowledge my husband, Ron Lacey, for supporting me and my writing in so many ways. If it were not for him, I would find it much, much more challenging to do my work in the world.

And to the entire team at BTSL, thank you. I appreciate what each one of you has done to bring this book to life and get it in readers' hands.

Nina Amir, the Inspiration to Creation Coach, is a 19X Amazon bestselling hybrid author. She supports writers on the journey to successful authorship as an Author Coach, Transformational Coach, and Certified High Performance Coach (CHPC®)—the only one working with writers.

Nina's most recent book, *Change the World One Book at a Time: Make a Positive and Meaningful Difference with Your Words*, was published in January 2026 by Books that Save Lives. Previously, she wrote three traditionally published books for aspiring authors—*How to Blog a Book*, *The Author Training Manual*, and *Creative Visualization for Writers*. Additionally, she has self-published a host of books and ebooks, including the Write Nonfiction NOW! series of guides. She has had 19 books on the Amazon Top 100 List and as many as six books on the Authorship bestseller list at the same time.

Nina is an award-winning journalist and blogger, as well as a successful nonfiction developmental editor. Some of her editing clients have sold 300,000+ copies of their books, landed deals with major publishing houses and created thriving businesses around their books.

To further support writers, Nina created the Nonfiction Writers' University, where members access a huge archive of resources, such as courses, ebooks, and interviews with writing and publishing experts, and receive monthly group Author Coaching. Additionally, she created the Write Nonfiction in November Challenge and Author of Change Transformational Programs.

Nina also founded the Inspired Creator Community, which provides group transformational (spiritual and personal growth) coaching around the topic of creating what matters. Many writers join this program to support their efforts to become authors.

You can read her three blogs, by visiting www.ninaamir.com. Find her writing-related blogs at writenonfictionnow.com and howtoblogabook.com as well.

Follow Nina on social media sites!

facebook.com/InspirationToCreation

instagram.com/inspirationToCreationCoach

youtube.com/ninaamir

tiktok.com/@inspiredcreator

bsky.app/profile/@ninaamir.bsky.social

x.com/ninaamir

linkedin.com/in/ninaamir

pinterest.com/ninaamir

Books That Save Lives came into being in 2024 when the editor and publisher, Brenda Knight, heard directly from readers and authors that certain self-help, grief, psychology books, and journals were providing a lifeline for folks. We live in a stressful world where it is increasingly difficult not to feel overwhelmed, worried, depressed, and downright scared. We intend to offer support for the vulnerable, including people struggling with mental wellness and physical illness as well as people of color, queer and trans adults and teens, immigrants and anyone who needs encouragement and inspiration.

From first responders, military veterans, and retirees to LGBTQ+ teens and to those experiencing the shock of bereavement and loss, our books have saved lives. To us, there is no higher calling.

We would love to hear from you! Our readers are our most important resource; we value your input, suggestions, and ideas.

Please stay in touch with us and follow us at:

www.booksthatsavelives.net

Instagram: @booksthatsavelives